Time Passages

By Robert Burtt & Bill Main

"The key to unlocking the door to our future opens with a journey into the past."

Robert Burtt & Bill Main

Fifth Printing

Dodgers
LAND CAMERA
AUTOMATIC 100
POLAROID

Craig Breedlove
SPIRIT OF AMERICA
SHELL
BOSTON
6
TRICK

JANUARY 1963

Poet Robert Frost, seen here receiving the "Congressional Medal" from President Kennedy during 1962, dies in Boston.

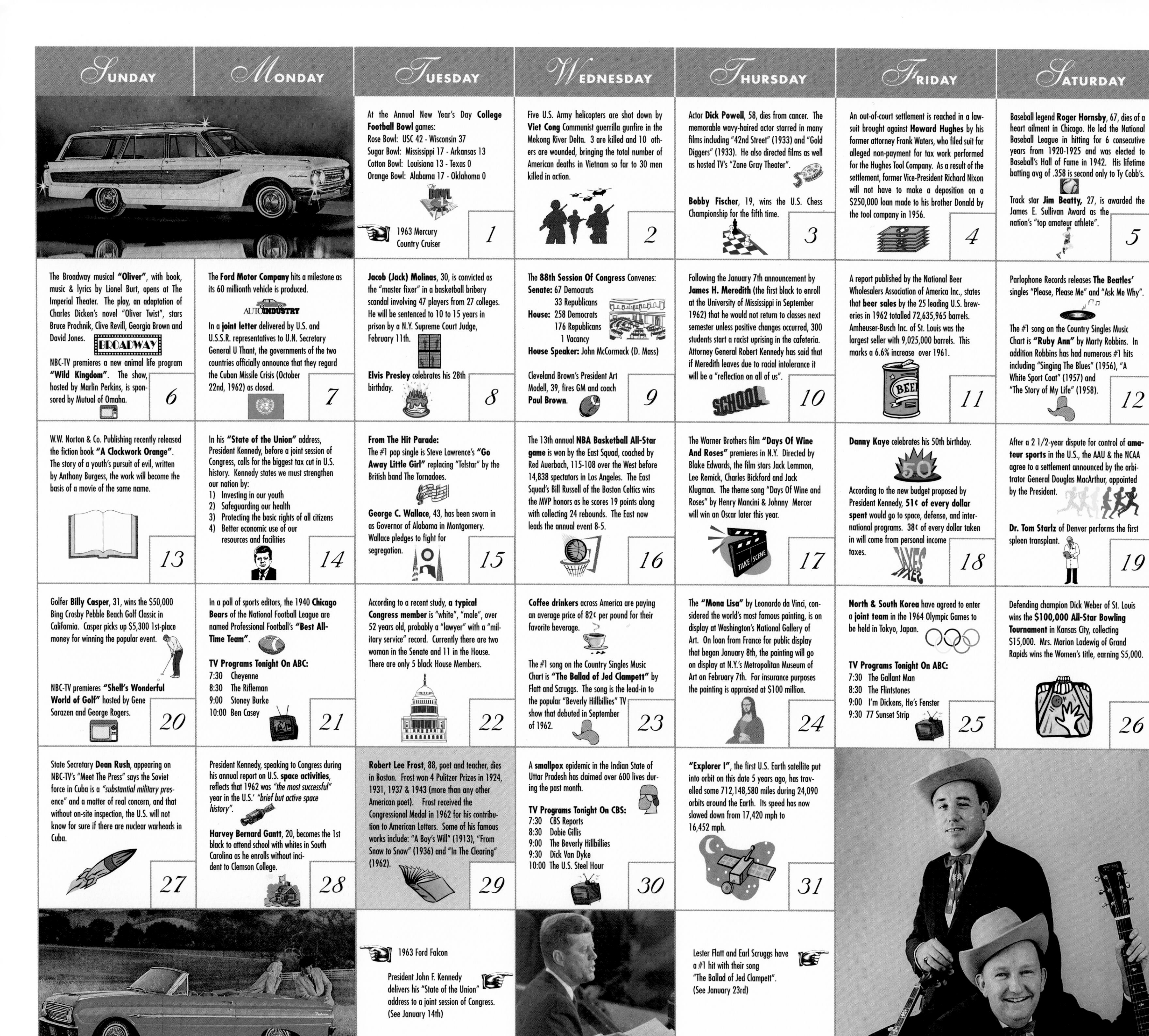

Sunday	Monday	Tuesday	Wednesday	Thursday	Friday	Saturday

1 — At the Annual New Year's Day **College Football Bowl** games:
Rose Bowl: USC 42 - Wisconsin 37
Sugar Bowl: Mississippi 17 - Arkansas 13
Cotton Bowl: Louisiana 13 - Texas 0
Orange Bowl: Alabama 17 - Oklahoma 0

1963 Mercury Country Cruiser

2 — Five U.S. Army helicopters are shot down by **Viet Cong** Communist guerrilla gunfire in the Mekong River Delta. 3 are killed and 10 others are wounded, bringing the total number of American deaths in Vietnam so far to 30 men killed in action.

3 — Actor **Dick Powell**, 58, dies from cancer. The memorable wavy-haired actor starred in many films including "42nd Street" (1933) and "Gold Diggers" (1933). He also directed films as well as hosted TV's "Zane Gray Theater".

Bobby Fischer, 19, wins the U.S. Chess Championship for the fifth time.

4 — An out-of-court settlement is reached in a lawsuit brought against **Howard Hughes** by his former attorney Frank Waters, who filed suit for alleged non-payment for tax work performed for the Hughes Tool Company. As a result of the settlement, former Vice-President Richard Nixon will not have to make a deposition on a $250,000 loan made to his brother Donald by the tool company in 1956.

5 — Baseball legend **Roger Hornsby**, 67, dies of a heart ailment in Chicago. He led the National Baseball League in hitting for 6 consecutive years from 1920-1925 and was elected to Baseball's Hall of Fame in 1942. His lifetime batting avg of .358 is second only to Ty Cobb's.

Track star **Jim Beatty**, 27, is awarded the James E. Sullivan Award as the nation's "top amateur athlete".

6 — The Broadway musical **"Oliver"**, with book, music & lyrics by Lionel Burt, opens at The Imperial Theater. The play, an adaptation of Charles Dicken's novel "Oliver Twist", stars Bruce Prochnik, Clive Revill, Georgia Brown and David Jones.

NBC-TV premieres a new animal life program **"Wild Kingdom"**. The show, hosted by Marlin Perkins, is sponsored by Mutual of Omaha.

7 — The **Ford Motor Company** hits a milestone as its 60 millionth vehicle is produced.

In a **joint letter** delivered by U.S. and U.S.S.R. representatives to U.N. Secretary General U Thant, the governments of the two countries officially announce that they regard the Cuban Missile Crisis (October 22nd, 1962) as closed.

8 — **Jacob (Jack) Molinas**, 30, is convicted as the "master fixer" in a basketball bribery scandal involving 47 players from 27 colleges. He will be sentenced to 10 to 15 years in prison by a N.Y. Supreme Court Judge, February 11th.

Elvis Presley celebrates his 28th birthday.

9 — The **88th Session Of Congress** Convenes:
Senate: 67 Democrats
33 Republicans
House: 258 Democrats
176 Republicans
1 Vacancy
House Speaker: John McCormack (D. Mass)

Cleveland Brown's President Art Modell, 39, fires GM and coach **Paul Brown**.

10 — Following the January 7th announcement by **James H. Meredith** (the first black to enroll at the University of Mississippi in September 1962) that he would not return to classes next semester unless positive changes occurred, 300 students start a racist uprising in the cafeteria. Attorney General Robert Kennedy has said that if Meredith leaves due to racial intolerance it will be a "reflection on all of us".

11 — A report published by the National Beer Wholesalers Association of America Inc., states that **beer sales** by the 25 leading U.S. breweries in 1962 totalled 72,635,965 barrels. Amheuser-Busch Inc. of St. Louis was the largest seller with 9,025,000 barrels. This marks a 6.6% increase over 1961.

12 — Parlophone Records releases **The Beatles'** singles "Please, Please Me" and "Ask Me Why".

The #1 song on the Country Singles Music Chart is **"Ruby Ann"** by Marty Robbins. In addition Robbins has had numerous #1 hits including "Singing The Blues" (1956), "A White Sport Coat" (1957) and "The Story of My Life" (1958).

13 — W.W. Norton & Co. Publishing recently released the fiction book **"A Clockwork Orange"**. The story of a youth's pursuit of evil, written by Anthony Burgess, the work will become the basis of a movie of the same name.

14 — In his **"State of the Union"** address, President Kennedy, before a joint session of Congress, calls for the biggest tax cut in U.S. history. Kennedy states we must strengthen our nation by:
1) Investing in our youth
2) Safeguarding our health
3) Protecting the basic rights of all citizens
4) Better economic use of our resources and facilities

15 — **From The Hit Parade:**
The #1 pop single is Steve Lawrence's **"Go Away Little Girl"** replacing "Telstar" by the British band The Tornadoes.

George C. Wallace, 43, has been sworn in as Governor of Alabama in Montgomery. Wallace pledges to fight for segregation.

16 — The 13th annual **NBA Basketball All-Star game** is won by the East Squad, coached by Red Auerbach, 115-108 over the West before 14,838 spectators in Los Angeles. The East Squad's Bill Russell of the Boston Celtics wins the MVP honors as he scores 19 points along with collecting 24 rebounds. The East now leads the annual event 8-5.

17 — The Warner Brothers film **"Days Of Wine And Roses"** premieres in N.Y. Directed by Blake Edwards, the film stars Jack Lemmon, Lee Remick, Charles Bickford and Jack Klugman. The theme song "Days Of Wine and Roses" by Henry Mancini & Johnny Mercer will win an Oscar later this year.

18 — **Danny Kaye** celebrates his 50th birthday.

According to the new budget proposed by President Kennedy, **51¢ of every dollar spent** would go to space, defense, and international programs. 38¢ of every dollar taken in will come from personal income taxes.

19 — After a 2 1/2-year dispute for control of **amateur sports** in the U.S., the AAU & the NCAA agree to a settlement announced by the arbitrator General Douglas MacArthur, appointed by the President.

Dr. Tom Starlz of Denver performs the first spleen transplant.

20 — Golfer **Billy Casper**, 31, wins the $50,000 Bing Crosby Pebble Beach Golf Classic in California. Casper picks up $5,300 1st-place money for winning the popular event.

NBC-TV premieres **"Shell's Wonderful World of Golf"** hosted by Gene Sarazen and George Rogers.

21 — In a poll of sports editors, the 1940 **Chicago Bears** of the National Football League are named Professional Football's **"Best All-Time Team"**.

TV Programs Tonight On ABC:
7:30 Cheyenne
8:30 The Rifleman
9:00 Stoney Burke
10:00 Ben Casey

22 — According to a recent study, **a typical Congress member** is "white", "male", over 52 years old, probably a "lawyer" with a "military service" record. Currently there are two woman in the Senate and 11 in the House. There are only 5 black House Members.

23 — **Coffee drinkers** across America are paying an average price of 82¢ per pound for their favorite beverage.

The #1 song on the Country Singles Music Chart is **"The Ballad of Jed Clampett"** by Flatt and Scruggs. The song is the lead-in to the popular "Beverly Hillbillies" TV show that debuted in September of 1962.

24 — The **"Mona Lisa"** by Leonardo da Vinci, considered the world's most famous painting, is on display at Washington's National Gallery of Art. On loan from France for public display that began January 8th, the painting will go on display at N.Y.'s Metropolitan Museum of Art on February 7th. For insurance purposes the painting is appraised at $100 million.

25 — **North & South Korea** have agreed to enter a **joint team** in the 1964 Olympic Games to be held in Tokyo, Japan.

TV Programs Tonight On ABC:
7:30 The Gallant Man
8:30 The Flintstones
9:00 I'm Dickens, He's Fenster
9:30 77 Sunset Strip

26 — Defending champion Dick Weber of St. Louis wins the **$100,000 All-Star Bowling Tournament** in Kansas City, collecting $15,000. Mrs. Marion Ladewig of Grand Rapids wins the Women's title, earning $5,000.

27 — State Secretary **Dean Rush**, appearing on NBC-TV's "Meet The Press" says the Soviet force in Cuba is a *"substantial military presence"* and a matter of real concern, and that without on-site inspection, the U.S. will not know for sure if there are nuclear warheads in Cuba.

28 — President Kennedy, speaking to Congress during his annual report on U.S. **space activities**, reflects that 1962 was *"the most successful"* year in the U.S.' *"brief but active space history"*.

Harvey Bernard Gantt, 20, becomes the 1st black to attend school with whites in South Carolina as he enrolls without incident to Clemson College.

29 — **Robert Lee Frost**, 88, poet and teacher, dies in Boston. Frost won 4 Pulitzer Prizes in 1924, 1931, 1937 & 1943 (more than any other American poet). Frost received the Congressional Medal in 1962 for his contribution to American Letters. Some of his famous works include: "A Boy's Will" (1913), "From Snow to Snow" (1936) and "In The Clearing" (1962).

30 — A **smallpox** epidemic in the Indian State of Uttar Pradesh has claimed over 600 lives during the past month.

TV Programs Tonight On CBS:
7:30 CBS Reports
8:30 Dobie Gillis
9:00 The Beverly Hillbillies
9:30 Dick Van Dyke
10:00 The U.S. Steel Hour

31 — **"Explorer I"**, the first U.S. Earth satellite put into orbit on this date 5 years ago, has travelled some 712,148,580 miles during 24,090 orbits around the Earth. Its speed has now slowed down from 17,420 mph to 16,452 mph.

1963 Ford Falcon

President John F. Kennedy delivers his "State of the Union" address to a joint session of Congress. (See January 14th)

Lester Flatt and Earl Scruggs have a #1 hit with their song "The Ballad of Jed Clampett". (See January 23rd)

FEBRUARY *1963*

Gregory Peck stars as an Alabama defense lawyer in the new film "To Kill A Mockingbird".

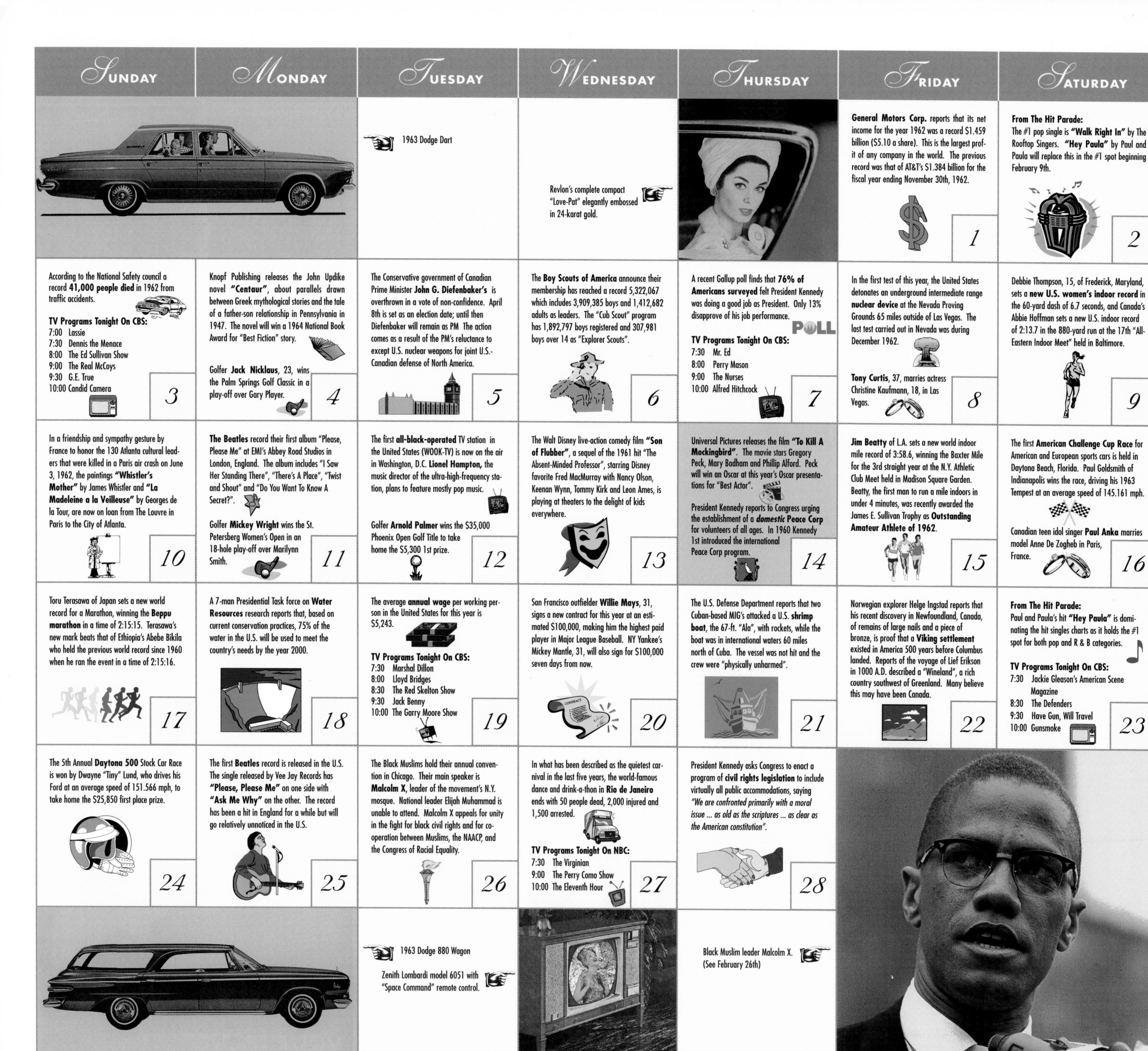

Sunday	Monday	Tuesday	Wednesday	Thursday	Friday	Saturday
		1963 Dodge Dart	Revlon's complete compact "Love-Pat" elegantly embossed in 24-karat gold.		**1** **General Motors Corp.** reports that its net income for the year 1962 was a record $1.459 billion ($5.10 a share). This is the largest profit of any company in the world. The previous record was that of AT&T's $1.384 billion for the fiscal year ending November 30th, 1962.	**2** **From The Hit Parade:** The #1 pop single is **"Walk Right In"** by The Rooftop Singers. **"Hey Paula"** by Paul and Paula will replace this in the #1 spot beginning February 9th.
3 According to the National Safety council a record **41,000 people died** in 1962 from traffic accidents. **TV Programs Tonight On CBS:** 7:00 Lassie 7:30 Dennis the Menace 8:00 The Ed Sullivan Show 9:00 The Real McCoys 9:30 G.E. True 10:00 Candid Camera	**4** Knopf Publishing releases the John Updike novel **"Centaur"**, about parallels drawn between Greek mythological stories and the tale of a father-son relationship in Pennsylvania in 1947. The novel will win a 1964 National Book Award for "Best Fiction" story. Golfer **Jack Nicklaus**, 23, wins the Palm Springs Golf Classic in a play-off over Gary Player.	**5** The Conservative government of Canadian Prime Minister **John G. Diefenbaker's** is overthrown in a vote of non-confidence. April 8th is set as an election date; until then Diefenbaker will remain as PM. The action comes as a result of the PM's reluctance to except U.S. nuclear weapons for joint U.S.-Canadian defense of North America.	**6** The **Boy Scouts of America** announce their membership has reached a record 5,322,067 which includes 3,909,385 boys and 1,412,682 adults as leaders. The "Cub Scout" program has 1,892,797 boys registered and 307,981 boys over 14 as "Explorer Scouts".	**7** A recent Gallup poll finds that **76% of Americans surveyed** felt President Kennedy was doing a good job as President. Only 13% disapprove of his job performance. POLL **TV Programs Tonight On CBS:** 7:30 Mr. Ed 8:00 Perry Mason 9:00 The Nurses 10:00 Alfred Hitchcock	**8** In the first test of this year, the United States detonates an underground intermediate range **nuclear device** at the Nevada Proving Grounds 65 miles outside of Las Vegas. The last test carried out in Nevada was during December 1962. **Tony Curtis**, 37, marries actress Christine Kaufmann, 18, in Las Vegas.	**9** Debbie Thompson, 15, of Frederick, Maryland, sets a **new U.S. women's indoor record** in the 60-yard dash of 6.7 seconds, and Canada's Abbie Hoffman sets a new U.S. indoor record of 2:13.7 in the 880-yard run at the 17th "All-Eastern Indoor Meet" held in Baltimore.
10 In a friendship and sympathy gesture by France to honor the 130 Atlanta cultural leaders that were killed in a Paris air crash on June 3, 1962, the paintings **"Whistler's Mother"** by James Whistler and **"La Madeleine a la Veilleuse"** by Georges de la Tour, are now on loan from The Louvre in Paris to the City of Atlanta.	**11** **The Beatles** record their first album "Please, Please Me" at EMI's Abbey Road Studios in London, England. The album includes "I Saw Her Standing There", "There's A Place", "Twist and Shout" and "Do You Want To Know A Secret?". Golfer **Mickey Wright** wins the St. Petersberg Women's Open in an 18-hole play-off over Marilynn Smith.	**12** The first **all-black-operated** TV station in the United States (WOOK-TV) is now on the air in Washington, D.C. **Lionel Hampton,** the music director of the ultra-high-frequency station, plans to feature mostly pop music. Golfer **Arnold Palmer** wins the $35,000 Phoenix Open Golf Title to take home the $5,300 1st prize.	**13** The Walt Disney live-action comedy film **"Son of Flubber"**, a sequel of the 1961 hit "The Absent-Minded Professor", starring Disney favorite Fred MacMurray with Nancy Olson, Keenan Wynn, Tommy Kirk and Leon Ames, is playing at theaters to the delight of kids everywhere.	**14** Universal Pictures releases the film **"To Kill A Mockingbird"**. The movie stars Gregory Peck, Mary Badham and Phillip Alford. Peck will win an Oscar at this year's Oscar presentations for "Best Actor". President Kennedy reports to Congress urging the establishment of a ***domestic* Peace Corp** for volunteers of all ages. In 1960 Kennedy 1st introduced the international Peace Corp program.	**15** **Jim Beatty** of L.A. sets a new world indoor mile record of 3:58.6, winning the Baxter Mile for the 3rd straight year at the N.Y. Athletic Club Meet held in Madison Square Garden. Beatty, the first man to run a mile indoors in under 4 minutes, was recently awarded the James E. Sullivan Trophy as **Outstanding Amateur Athlete of 1962.**	**16** The first **American Challenge Cup Race** for American and European sports cars is held in Daytona Beach, Florida. Paul Goldsmith of Indianapolis wins the race, driving his 1963 Tempest at an average speed of 145.161 mph. Canadian teen idol singer **Paul Anka** marries model Anne De Zogheb in Paris, France.
17 Toru Terasawa of Japan sets a new world record for a Marathon, winning the **Beppu marathon** in a time of 2:15:15. Terasawa's new mark beats that of Ethiopia's Abebe Bikila who held the previous world record since 1960 when he ran the event in a time of 2:15:16.	**18** A 7-man Presidential Task force on **Water Resources** research reports that, based on current conservation practices, 75% of the water in the U.S. will be used to meet the country's needs by the year 2000.	**19** The average **annual wage** per working person in the United States for this year is $5,243. **TV Programs Tonight On CBS:** 7:30 Marshal Dillon 8:00 Lloyd Bridges 8:30 The Red Skelton Show 9:30 Jack Benny 10:00 The Garry Moore Show	**20** San Francisco outfielder **Willie Mays**, 31, signs a new contract for this year at an estimated $100,000, making him the highest paid player in Major League Baseball. NY Yankee's Mickey Mantle, 31, will also sign for $100,000 seven days from now. CONTRACT	**21** The U.S. Defense Department reports that two Cuban-based MIG's attacked a U.S. **shrimp boat**, the 67-ft. "Ala", with rockets, while the boat was in international waters 60 miles north of Cuba. The vessel was not hit and the crew were "physically unharmed".	**22** Norwegian explorer Helge Ingstad reports that his recent discovery in Newfoundland, Canada, of remains of large nails and a piece of bronze, is proof that a **Viking settlement** existed in America 500 years before Columbus landed. Reports of the voyage of Lief Erikson in 1000 A.D. described a "Wineland", a rich country southwest of Greenland. Many believe this may have been Canada.	**23** **From The Hit Parade:** Paul and Paula's hit **"Hey Paula"** is dominating the hit singles charts as it holds the #1 spot for both pop and R & B categories. **TV Programs Tonight On CBS:** 7:30 Jackie Gleason's American Scene Magazine 8:30 The Defenders 9:30 Have Gun, Will Travel 10:00 Gunsmoke
24 The 5th Annual **Daytona 500** Stock Car Race is won by Dwayne "Tiny" Lund, who drives his Ford at an average speed of 151.566 mph, to take home the $25,850 first place prize.	**25** The first **Beatles** record is released in the U.S. The single released by Vee Jay Records has **"Please, Please Me"** on one side with **"Ask Me Why"** on the other. The record has been a hit in England for a while but will go relatively unnoticed in the U.S.	**26** The Black Muslims hold their annual convention in Chicago. Their main speaker is **Malcolm X**, leader of the movement's N.Y. mosque. National leader Elijah Muhammad is unable to attend. Malcolm X appeals for unity in the fight for black civil rights and for co-operation between Muslims, the NAACP, and the Congress of Racial Equality.	**27** In what has been described as the quietest carnival in the last five years, the world-famous dance and drink-a-thon in **Rio de Janeiro** ends with 50 people dead, 2,000 injured and 1,500 arrested. **TV Programs Tonight On NBC:** 7:30 The Virginian 9:00 The Perry Como Show 10:00 The Eleventh Hour	**28** President Kennedy asks Congress to enact a program of **civil rights legislation** to include virtually all public accommodations, saying *"We are confronted primarily with a moral issue ... as old as the scriptures ... as clear as the American constitution"*.		
		1963 Dodge 880 Wagon Zenith Lombardi model 6051 with "Space Command" remote control.		Black Muslim leader Malcolm X. (See February 26th)		

MARCH 1963

Elvis Presley stars in the new film "Kid Galahad".

Sunday	Monday	Tuesday	Wednesday	Thursday	Friday	Saturday

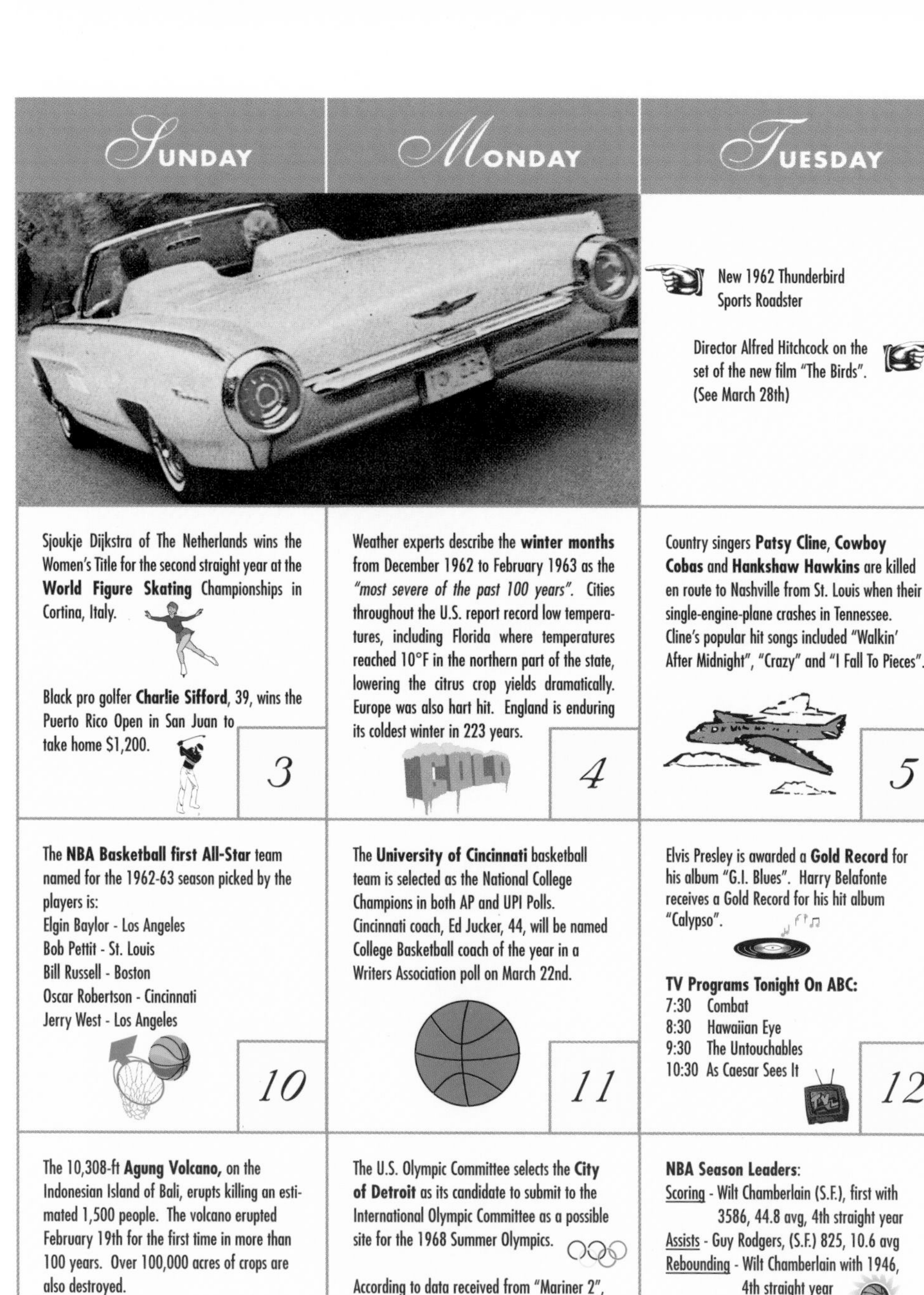

New 1962 Thunderbird Sports Roadster

Director Alfred Hitchcock on the set of the new film "The Birds". (See March 28th)

1 — The National Center for Atmospheric Research in Palestine, Texas, sails a **telescope-carrying balloon** to an altitude of 77,000 feet above 96% of the Earth's atmosphere to check Mars to see if it could support life.

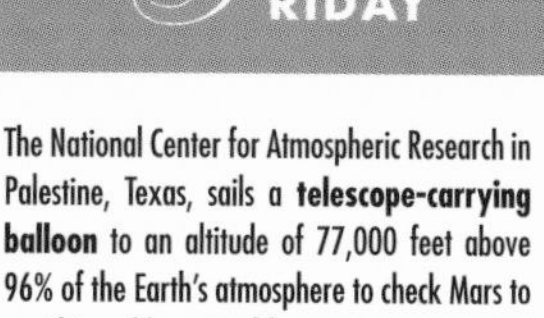

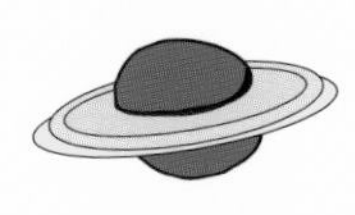

2 — **From The Hit Parade:**
The #1 pop song is "Walk Like A Man" by the Four Seasons.

TV Programs Tonight On ABC:
7:30 The Roy Rogers and Dale Evans Show
8:30 Mr. Smith Goes to Washington
9:00 The Lawrence Welk Show
10:00 Saturday Night "Fight of the Week"

3 — Sjoukje Dijkstra of The Netherlands wins the Women's Title for the second straight year at the **World Figure Skating** Championships in Cortina, Italy.

Black pro golfer **Charlie Sifford**, 39, wins the Puerto Rico Open in San Juan to take home $1,200.

4 — Weather experts describe the **winter months** from December 1962 to February 1963 as the *"most severe of the past 100 years"*. Cities throughout the U.S. report record low temperatures, including Florida where temperatures reached 10°F in the northern part of the state, lowering the citrus crop yields dramatically. Europe was also hart hit. England is enduring its coldest winter in 223 years.

5 — Country singers **Patsy Cline**, **Cowboy Cobas** and **Hankshaw Hawkins** are killed en route to Nashville from St. Louis when their single-engine-plane crashes in Tennessee. Cline's popular hit songs included "Walkin' After Midnight", "Crazy" and "I Fall To Pieces".

6 — Greenwood, Mississippi: Four black voter registration workers are **shot and wounded** by a group of unidentified whites. This incident will be followed by many more such actions during the coming months during a major black voter registration campaign.

Ed McMahon celebrates his 40th birthday.

7 — The world's largest commercial office building, the $100 million **Pan-Am Building** in New York City, is dedicated. The 59-story, 808-ft structure has 2.4 million square feet of floor space.

8 — Columbia Pictures releases the film **"The War Lover"**, the story of a troubled World War II combat pilot. Based on the novel by John Hersey, the film stars Steve McQueen, Robert Wagner & Shirley Anne Fields.

9 — The U.S. State Department answers to Soviet charges that the U.S. in South Vietnam are using **asphyxiation gases** and **noxious chemicals** in fighting the Viet Cong. The State Department replies *"We have never used poison gas in South Vietnam and there is no truth in communist reports that we are using it now"*.

10 — The **NBA Basketball first All-Star** team named for the 1962-63 season picked by the players is:
Elgin Baylor - Los Angeles
Bob Pettit - St. Louis
Bill Russell - Boston
Oscar Robertson - Cincinnati
Jerry West - Los Angeles

11 — The **University of Cincinnati** basketball team is selected as the National College Champions in both AP and UPI Polls. Cincinnati coach, Ed Jucker, 44, will be named College Basketball coach of the year in a Writers Association poll on March 22nd.

12 — Elvis Presley is awarded a **Gold Record** for his album "G.I. Blues". Harry Belafonte receives a Gold Record for his hit album "Calypso".

TV Programs Tonight On ABC:
7:30 Combat
8:30 Hawaiian Eye
9:30 The Untouchables
10:30 As Caesar Sees It

13 — The Men's & Women's **U.S. Volleyball** Association All-American teams include:
The Men's Team:
Mike O'Hara, Barry Brown, Walt Schiller, Mike Bright, Charles Nelson and Pedro Velasco
The Women's Team:
Jane Ward, Jean Gaertner, Pat Lucas, Nancy Owen, Lou Fara Clark, and Beverly Miller

14 — The **NBA Podoloff Cup**, awarded to Basketball's Most Valuable Player for the third consecutive year and fourth time in six seasons is awarded to Boston Celtic center, star Bill Russell.

15 — In the first known incident, two Soviet reconnaissance planes **violate U.S. airspace** when they fly over Alaska. USAF-102 jet fighters are sent up from Alaskan bases and track the Soviet planes on radar, without closing to within visual distance or taking any hostile action.

16 — Elvis Presley plays a singing boxer in the United Artists film **"Kid Galahad"**, with Gig Young, Lola Albright and Joan Blackman is now playing at theaters around the country.

17 — The 10,308-ft **Agung Volcano,** on the Indonesian Island of Bali, erupts killing an estimated 1,500 people. The volcano erupted February 19th for the first time in more than 100 years. Over 100,000 acres of crops are also destroyed.

18 — The U.S. Olympic Committee selects the **City of Detroit** as its candidate to submit to the International Olympic Committee as a possible site for the 1968 Summer Olympics.

According to data received from "Mariner 2", the planet **Venus has surface temperatures that exceed 800°F.** The probe passed Venus in December of 1962 scanning the planet from 21,648 miles.

19 — **NBA Season Leaders:**
Scoring - Wilt Chamberlain (S.F.), first with 3586, 44.8 avg, 4th straight year
Assists - Guy Rodgers, (S.F.) 825, 10.6 avg
Rebounding - Wilt Chamberlain with 1946, 4th straight year

President Kennedy concludes two days of meetings in Costa Rica with six other Central American Presidents.

20 — CBS-TV 9:00pm: The #1-rated show in the nation is **"The Beverly Hillbillies"** starring Buddy Ebsen, Irene Ryan, Donna Douglas and Max Baer.

According to Government statistics, there are now **2 million fewer farms** in the United States than there were in 1950. the Agriculture Department announces there are now 3.6 million farms around the nation.

21 — **Alcatraz**, the famous maximum security penitentiary located on an island in San Francisco Bay, closes its doors 39 years after it opened on June 19th, 1934. Attorney General Robert Kennedy is on hand to close the prison and Frank Watherman is the last prisoner to leave the island.

22 — EMI-Parlophone Records releases **The Beatles** first album "Please, Please Me" in England. Within 3 weeks the album hit #1 in the United Kingdom.

TV Programs Tonight On CBS:
7:30 Rawhide
8:30 Route 66
9:30 Fair Exchange
10:30 Eyewitness

23 — Louisville, Kentucky: Loyola defeats Cincinnati 60-58 in overtime to win the **NCAA Basketball Championship**. Loyola was the highest-scoring team in the nation with an average 91.8 pts per game. Third place Duke's Art Heyman wins the MVP.

Providence defeats Canisius 81-66 at the NIT tournament finals in N.Y. Ray Flynn of Providence wins the MVP.

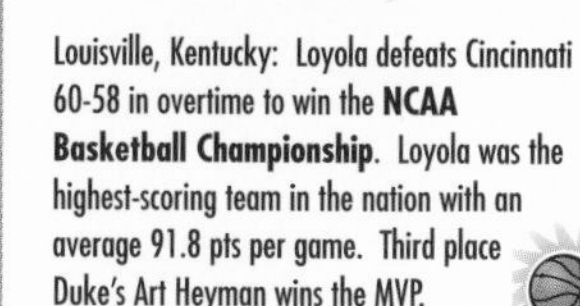

24 — **From The Hit Parade:**
The #1 pop album is Frank Fontaine's **"Songs I Sing On The Gleason Show"** which will remain #1 for the next 5 weeks. The #1 pop single is **"Our Day Will Come"** by Ruby and The Romantics.

25 — Former World Featherweight Boxing Champion, **Davey Moore**, 29, dies 4 days after collapsing into a coma in his dressing room following his loss to Ultiminio Ramos of Cuba in Los Angeles on March 21st.

26 — **NHL Season Leaders:**
Points: Gordie Howe (Detroit) 2nd time with 38 goals, 48 assists for 86 points
Goals - Gordie Howe 5th time 38
Assists - Henri Richard (Mtl) 2nd time 50
Goals-Against Avg - Jacques Plante (Mtl) 2.49 2nd straight, 7th time
Penalty Minutes - Howie Young (Det) with a record 273

27 — MGM's star-studded movie **"How The West Was Won"** premieres in N.Y.C. Directed by John Ford, the film stars James Stewart, Gregory Peck, Debbie Reynolds, Richard Widmark, Thelma Ritter, John Wayne, Henry Fonda and Carol Baker. James Webb will win an Oscar for "Best Screenplay".

28 — Universal Pictures releases a new film about birds who attack a town in the Alfred Hitchcock thriller **"The Birds"**. The movie stars Tippi Hedren, Rod Taylor, Jessica Tandy and Suzanne Pleshette.

29 — The California Medical Association is the first group to publicly declare that **cigarette smoking** is hazardous to your health.

American smokers are paying an average price of 26¢ per pack of cigarettes.

30 — NASA selects 15 more pilots to train to become **astronauts**, starting June 17th as members of the 4th class of the Aerospace Research Pilots course at Edwards AF Base, California. AF Capt. Edward J. Dwight Jr., 29, becomes the first black chosen for the program.

31 — Glenn "Fireball" Roberts wins the **Southeastern 500** Late Model Stock Car Race in Bristol, Tennessee, driving a 1963 Ford.

TV Programs Tonight On ABC:
7:00 Father Knows Best
7:30 The Jetsons
8:00 Sunday Night ABC Movie
10:00 Voice of Firestone
10:30 Howard K. Smith

1963 Volkswagen Station Wagon sells for $2,655.

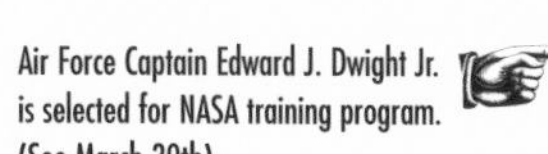

Air Force Captain Edward J. Dwight Jr. is selected for NASA training program. (See March 30th)

APRIL 1963

"Best Supporting Actress" Patty Duke celebrates her Oscar win with her co-manager Mrs. Ethel Ross.

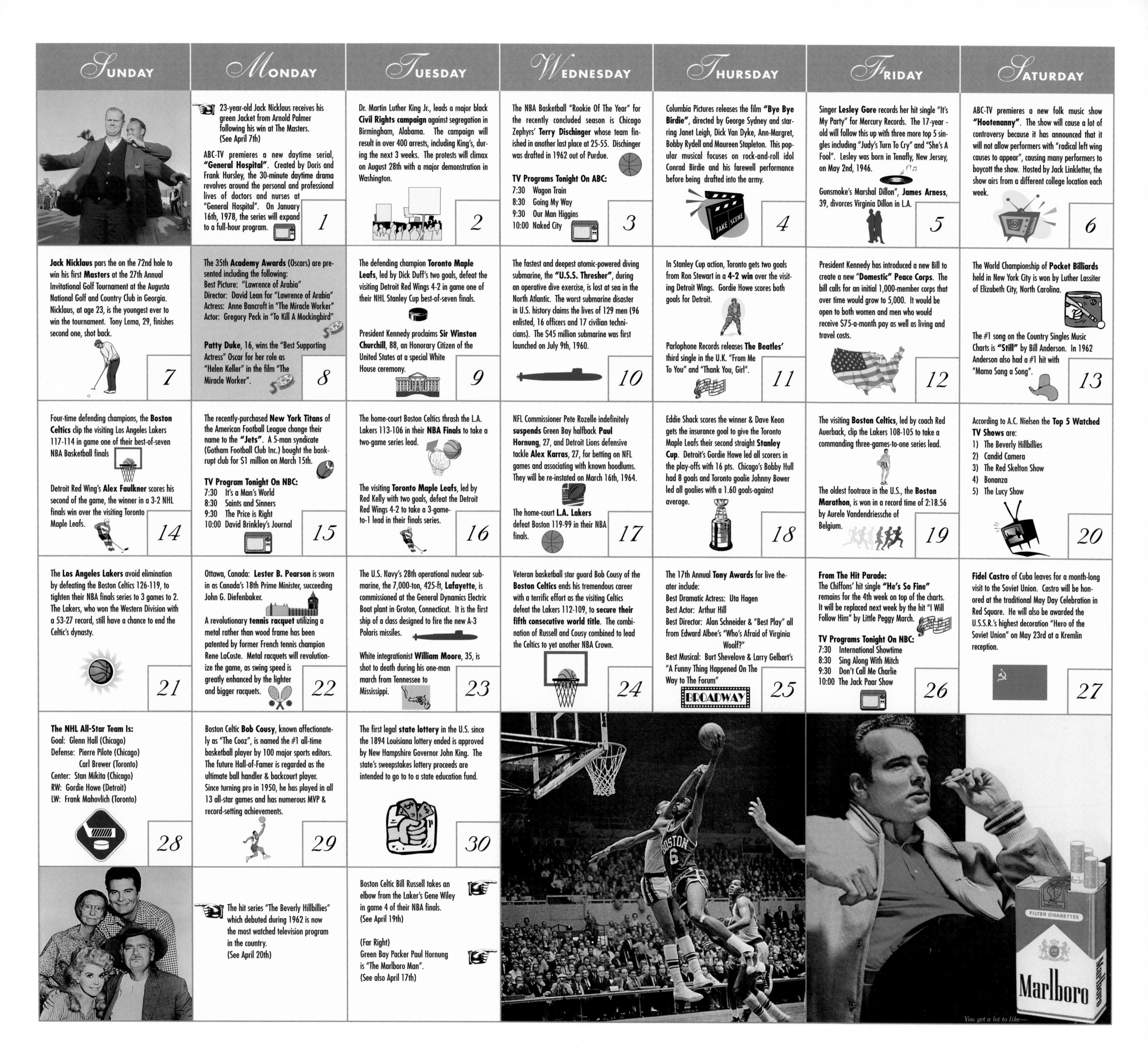

Sunday	Monday	Tuesday	Wednesday	Thursday	Friday	Saturday

1 — 23-year-old Jack Nicklaus receives his green Jacket from Arnold Palmer following his win at The Masters. (See April 7th)

ABC-TV premieres a new daytime serial, **"General Hospital"**. Created by Doris and Frank Hursley, the 30-minute daytime drama revolves around the personal and professional lives of doctors and nurses at "General Hospital". On January 16th, 1978, the series will expand to a full-hour program.

2 — Dr. Martin Luther King Jr., leads a major black **Civil Rights campaign** against segregation in Birmingham, Alabama. The campaign will result in over 400 arrests, including King's, during the next 3 weeks. The protests will climax on August 28th with a major demonstration in Washington.

3 — The NBA Basketball "Rookie Of The Year" for the recently concluded season is Chicago Zephyrs' **Terry Dischinger** whose team finished in another last place at 25-55. Dischinger was drafted in 1962 out of Purdue.

TV Programs Tonight On ABC:
7:30 Wagon Train
8:30 Going My Way
9:30 Our Man Higgins
10:00 Naked City

4 — Columbia Pictures releases the film **"Bye Bye Birdie"**, directed by George Sydney and starring Janet Leigh, Dick Van Dyke, Ann-Margret, Bobby Rydell and Maureen Stapleton. This popular musical focuses on rock-and-roll idol Conrad Birdie and his farewell performance before being drafted into the army.

5 — Singer **Lesley Gore** records her hit single "It's My Party" for Mercury Records. The 17-year-old will follow this up with three more top 5 singles including "Judy's Turn To Cry" and "She's A Fool". Lesley was born in Tenafly, New Jersey, on May 2nd, 1946.

Gunsmoke's Marshal Dillon", **James Arness**, 39, divorces Virginia Dillon in L.A.

6 — ABC-TV premieres a new folk music show **"Hootenanny"**. The show will cause a lot of controversy because it has announced that it will not allow performers with "radical left wing causes to appear", causing many performers to boycott the show. Hosted by Jack Linkletter, the show airs from a different college location each week.

7 — **Jack Nicklaus** pars the on the 72nd hole to win his first **Masters** at the 27th Annual Invitational Golf Tournament at the Augusta National Golf and Country Club in Georgia. Nicklaus, at age 23, is the youngest ever to win the tournament. Tony Lema, 29, finishes second one, shot back.

8 — The 35th **Academy Awards** (Oscars) are presented including the following:
Best Picture: "Lawrence of Arabia"
Director: David Lean for "Lawrence of Arabia"
Actress: Anne Bancroft in "The Miracle Worker"
Actor: Gregory Peck in "To Kill A Mockingbird"

Patty Duke, 16, wins the "Best Supporting Actress" Oscar for her role as "Helen Keller" in the film "The Miracle Worker".

9 — The defending champion **Toronto Maple Leafs**, led by Dick Duff's two goals, defeat the visiting Detroit Red Wings 4-2 in game one of their NHL Stanley Cup best-of-seven finals.

President Kennedy proclaims **Sir Winston Churchill**, 88, an Honorary Citizen of the United States at a special White House ceremony.

10 — The fastest and deepest atomic-powered diving submarine, the **"U.S.S. Thresher"**, during an operative dive exercise, is lost at sea in the North Atlantic. The worst submarine disaster in U.S. history claims the lives of 129 men (96 enlisted, 16 officers and 17 civilian technicians). The $45 million submarine was first launched on July 9th, 1960.

11 — In Stanley Cup action, Toronto gets two goals from Ron Stewart in a **4-2 win** over the visiting Detroit Wings. Gordie Howe scores both goals for Detroit.

Parlophone Records releases **The Beatles'** third single in the U.K. "From Me To You" and "Thank You, Girl".

12 — President Kennedy has introduced a new Bill to create a new **"Domestic" Peace Corps**. The bill calls for an initial 1,000-member corps that over time would grow to 5,000. It would be open to both women and men who would receive $75-a-month pay as well as living and travel costs.

13 — The World Championship of **Pocket Billiards** held in New York City is won by Luther Lassiter of Elizabeth City, North Carolina.

The #1 song on the Country Singles Music Charts is **"Still"** by Bill Anderson. In 1962 Anderson also had a #1 hit with "Mama Sang a Song".

14 — Four-time defending champions, the **Boston Celtics** clip the visiting Los Angeles Lakers 117-114 in game one of their best-of-seven NBA Basketball finals

Detroit Red Wing's **Alex Faulkner** scores his second of the game, the winner in a 3-2 NHL finals win over the visiting Toronto Maple Leafs.

15 — The recently-purchased **New York Titans** of the American Football League change their name to the **"Jets"**. A 5-man syndicate (Gotham Football Club Inc.) bought the bankrupt club for $1 million on March 15th.

TV Program Tonight On NBC:
7:30 It's a Man's World
8:30 Saints and Sinners
9:30 The Price is Right
10:00 David Brinkley's Journal

16 — The home-court Boston Celtics thrash the L.A. Lakers 113-106 in their **NBA Finals** to take a two-game series lead.

The visiting **Toronto Maple Leafs**, led by Red Kelly with two goals, defeat the Detroit Red Wings 4-2 to take a 3-game-to-1 lead in their finals series.

17 — NFL Commissioner Pete Rozelle indefinitely **suspends** Green Bay halfback **Paul Hornung**, 27, and Detroit Lions defensive tackle **Alex Karras**, 27, for betting on NFL games and associating with known hoodlums. They will be re-instated on March 16th, 1964.

The home-court **L.A. Lakers** defeat Boston 119-99 in their NBA finals.

18 — Eddie Shack scores the winner & Dave Keon gets the insurance goal to give the Toronto Maple Leafs their second straight **Stanley Cup**. Detroit's Gordie Howe led all scorers in the play-offs with 16 pts. Chicago's Bobby Hull had 8 goals and Toronto goalie Johnny Bower led all goalies with a 1.60 goals-against average.

19 — The visiting **Boston Celtics**, led by coach Red Auerback, clip the Lakers 108-105 to take a commanding three-games-to-one series lead.

The oldest footrace in the U.S., the **Boston Marathon**, is won in a record time of 2:18.56 by Aurele Vandendriessche of Belgium.

20 — According to A.C. Nielsen the **Top 5 Watched TV Shows** are:
1) The Beverly Hillbillies
2) Candid Camera
3) The Red Skelton Show
4) Bonanza
5) The Lucy Show

21 — The **Los Angeles Lakers** avoid elimination by defeating the Boston Celtics 126-119, to tighten their NBA finals series to 3 games to 2. The Lakers, who won the Western Division with a 53-27 record, still have a chance to end the Celtic's dynasty.

22 — Ottawa, Canada: **Lester B. Pearson** is sworn in as Canada's 18th Prime Minister, succeeding John G. Diefenbaker.

A revolutionary **tennis racquet** utilizing a metal rather than wood frame has been patented by former French tennis champion Rene LaCoste. Metal racquets will revolutionize the game, as swing speed is greatly enhanced by the lighter and bigger racquets.

23 — The U.S. Navy's 28th operational nuclear submarine, the 7,000-ton, 425-ft, **Lafayette**, is commissioned at the General Dynamics Electric Boat plant in Groton, Connecticut. It is the first ship of a class designed to fire the new A-3 Polaris missiles.

White integrationist **William Moore**, 35, is shot to death during his one-man march from Tennessee to Mississippi.

24 — Veteran basketball star guard Bob Cousy of the **Boston Celtics** ends his tremendous career with a terrific effort as the visiting Celtics defeat the Lakers 112-109, to **secure their fifth consecutive world title**. The combination of Russell and Cousy combined to lead the Celtics to yet another NBA Crown.

25 — The 17th Annual **Tony Awards** for live theater include:
Best Dramatic Actress: Uta Hagen
Best Actor: Arthur Hill
Best Director: Alan Schneider & "Best Play" all from Edward Albee's "Who's Afraid of Virginia Woolf?"
Best Musical: Burt Shevelove & Larry Gelbart's "A Funny Thing Happened On The Way to The Forum"

26 — **From The Hit Parade:**
The Chiffons' hit single **"He's So Fine"** remains for the 4th week on top of the charts. It will be replaced next week by the hit "I Will Follow Him" by Little Peggy March.

TV Programs Tonight On NBC:
7:30 International Showtime
8:30 Sing Along With Mitch
9:30 Don't Call Me Charlie
10:00 The Jack Paar Show

27 — **Fidel Castro** of Cuba leaves for a month-long visit to the Soviet Union. Castro will be honored at the traditional May Day Celebration in Red Square. He will also be awarded the U.S.S.R.'s highest decoration "Hero of the Soviet Union" on May 23rd at a Kremlin reception.

28 — **The NHL All-Star Team Is:**
Goal: Glenn Hall (Chicago)
Defense: Pierre Pilote (Chicago)
Carl Brewer (Toronto)
Center: Stan Mikita (Chicago)
RW: Gordie Howe (Detroit)
LW: Frank Mahovlich (Toronto)

29 — Boston Celtic **Bob Cousy**, known affectionately as "The Cooz", is named the #1 all-time basketball player by 100 major sports editors. The future Hall-of-Famer is regarded as the ultimate ball handler & backcourt player. Since turning pro in 1950, he has played in all 13 all-star games and has numerous MVP & record-setting achievements.

30 — The first legal **state lottery** in the U.S. since the 1894 Louisiana lottery ended is approved by New Hampshire Governor John King. The state's sweepstakes lottery proceeds are intended to go to to a state education fund.

The hit series "The Beverly Hillbillies" which debuted during 1962 is now the most watched television program in the country. (See April 20th)

Boston Celtic Bill Russell takes an elbow from the Laker's Gene Wiley in game 4 of their NBA finals. (See April 19th)

(Far Right) Green Bay Packer Paul Hornung is "The Marlboro Man". (See also April 17th)

MAY

Astronaut Gordon Cooper, aboard "Faith 7", completes the longest U.S. space flight in history.

Sunday	Monday	Tuesday	Wednesday	Thursday	Friday	Saturday

Polaroid Automatic 100 Land Camera gives color pictures in only 50 seconds.

Shirley Booth wins a "Best Actress" Emmy for her role in the hit TV series "Hazel". (See May 26th)

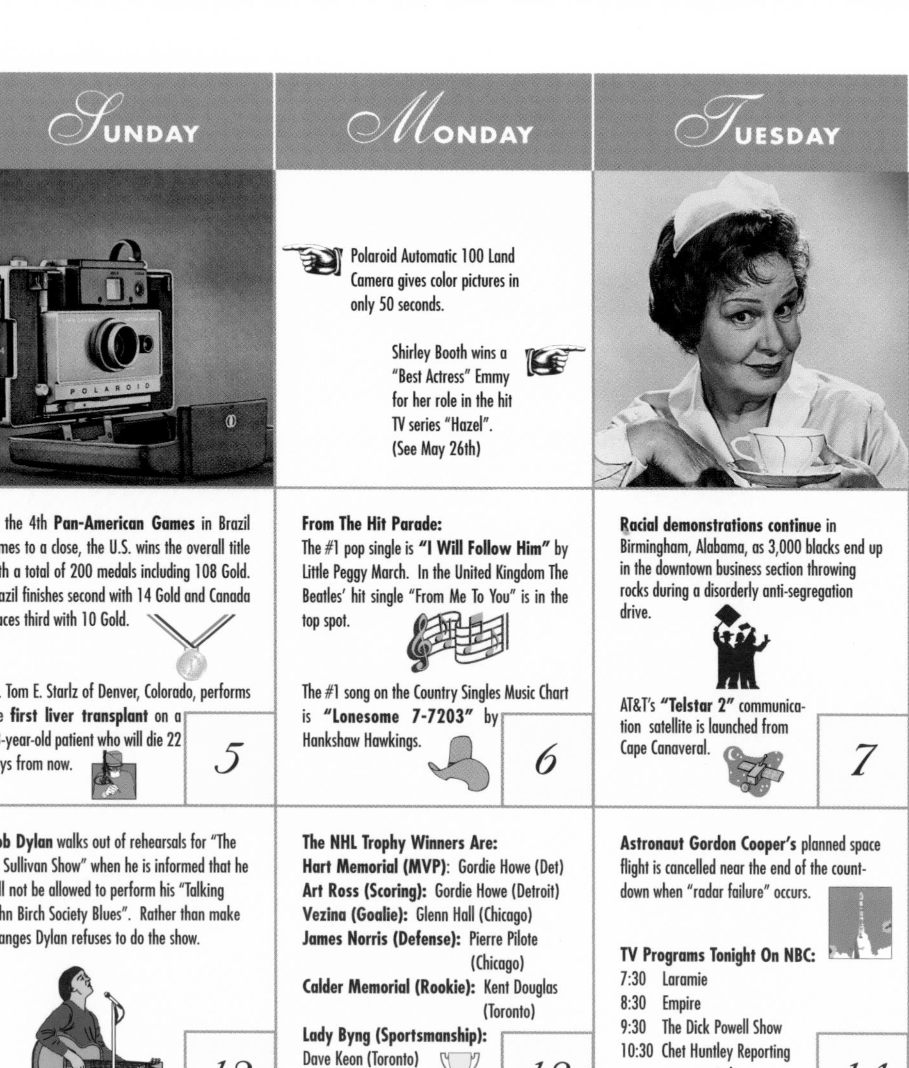

1

A group of 8 black integrationists **are arrested** in Alabama while attempting to complete the "Freedom Walk" initiated by white marcher William Moore, who was shot and killed in Alabama on April 24th en route to Jackson where he planned to present his integration appeal to Governor Ross Barnett.

2

Civil rights leaders step up their protests for equal rights in many cities. During the next week, over 2,500 demonstrators, including children, will be arrested. Police use dogs and fire hoses to break up the marches.

Former Vice-President Nixon joins the N.Y. law firm of Mudge, Stern, Baldwin and Todd.

3

A new Broadway musical comedy, **"She Loves Me"**, is playing at the Eugene O'Neill Theater, starring Barbara Cook, Daniel Massey, Barbara Baxley, Nathaniel Frey & Jack Cassidy who will win a Tony Award for "Best Supporting Actor in a Musical". The play is written by Joe Masteroff.

BROADWAY

4

The chestnut colt **"Chateaugay"** with jockey Braulio Braez aboard wins the 89th **Kentucky Derby** in a time of 2:01 4/5 on a fast track, edging **"Never Bend"** to capture the $151,400 first prize. The 1962 race record time of 2:00 2/5 set by "Decidedly" remains intact. "Candy Spots" finishes third.

Comedienne **Carol Burnett**, 28, marries TV producer Joseph Hamilton in Mexico.

5

As the 4th **Pan-American Games** in Brazil comes to a close, the U.S. wins the overall title with a total of 200 medals including 108 Gold. Brazil finishes second with 14 Gold and Canada places third with 10 Gold.

Dr. Tom E. Starlz of Denver, Colorado, performs the **first liver transplant** on a 48-year-old patient who will die 22 days from now.

6

From The Hit Parade:
The #1 pop single is **"I Will Follow Him"** by Little Peggy March. In the United Kingdom The Beatles' hit single "From Me To You" is in the top spot.

The #1 song on the Country Singles Music Chart is **"Lonesome 7-7203"** by Hankshaw Hawkings.

7

Racial demonstrations continue in Birmingham, Alabama, as 3,000 blacks end up in the downtown business section throwing rocks during a disorderly anti-segregation drive.

AT&T's **"Telstar 2"** communication satellite is launched from Cape Canaveral.

8

St. Louis Cardinal outfielder **Stan Musial** sets a "extra-base record" when he hits a home run against the L.A. Dodgers in St. Louis. The record now stands at 1,357, which includes 717 doubles, 175 triples, and 465 home runs.

Reverend Martin L. King Jr. is convicted in Birmingham of having paraded on Good Friday without a permit. The penalty imposed is 180 days in jail plus a $100 fine.

9

International Brotherhood of Teamsters President **James Hoffa** is indicted by a Federal Grand Jury in Nashville, Tennessee, on charges of "jury tampering" during his 1962 trial that ended in a mistrial.

TV Programs Tonight On ABC:
7:30 Ozzie and Harriet
8:00 Donna Reed
8:30 Leave It To Beaver
9:00 My Three Sons

10

Pittsburgh Steeler football star, defensive tackle **Gene "Big Daddy" Lipscomb**, 31, is found dead of an apparent heroine overdose in Baltimore.

From the Hit Parade:
The top album in the U.S. is "Days Of Wine and Roses" by Andy Williams.

11

Left-handed pitching ace **Sandy Koufax**, 27, of the L.A. Dodgers tosses a superb ***no-hitter*** against the visiting San Francisco Giants in an 8-0 victory. The *no-hitter* is the second of Koufax's career.

12

Bob Dylan walks out of rehearsals for "The Ed Sullivan Show" when he is informed that he will not be allowed to perform his "Talking John Birch Society Blues". Rather than make changes Dylan refuses to do the show.

13

The NHL Trophy Winners Are:
Hart Memorial (MVP): Gordie Howe (Det)
Art Ross (Scoring): Gordie Howe (Detroit)
Vezina (Goalie): Glenn Hall (Chicago)
James Norris (Defense): Pierre Pilote (Chicago)
Calder Memorial (Rookie): Kent Douglas (Toronto)
Lady Byng (Sportsmanship): Dave Keon (Toronto)

14

Astronaut Gordon Cooper's planned space flight is cancelled near the end of the count-down when "radar failure" occurs.

TV Programs Tonight On NBC:
7:30 Laramie
8:30 Empire
9:30 The Dick Powell Show
10:30 Chet Huntley Reporting

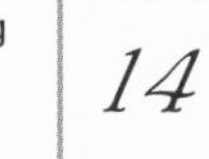

15

The 5th Annual **Grammy Awards are presented to:**
Record Of The Year: Tony Bennett for "I Left My Heart In San Francisco"
Best Performance by a Vocal Group: Peter, Paul and Mary for "If I Had A Hammer"
Best R & B: Ray Charles for "I Can't Stop Loving You"

16

Astronaut **Gordon Cooper**, 36, becomes the 1st American to stay in space more than a day (34 hr, 19 min, 49 sec) during the last of the Mercury flights, "Faith 7". Due to a malfunction in the craft's automatic control system, Cooper is forced to go to manual control during re-entry.

17

The second MLB *no-hitter* for this season is registered by right-handed pitcher **Don Nottebart**, 27, of the Houston Colts as he hurls a *no-hit* 4-1 win over the Philadelphia Phillies in Houston. Philadelphia's run was unearned.

TV Programs Tonight On NBC:
8:30 Doctor Kildare
9:30 Hazel
10:00 The Andy Williams Show

18

"Candy Spots" with jockey Willie Shoemaker aboard wins the **Preakness Stakes** Horse Race with **"Chateaugay"** coming in second and "Never Bend" in third.

Syracuse's **Ernie Davis**, winner of the 1961 "Heisman Trophy", the first black recipient of College football's outstanding player award, dies of leukemia.

19

The first **Monterey Folk Festival** comes to an end. The three-day concert included performances by Joan Baez, Bob Dylan, Pete Seeger, Peter, Paul and Mary, and The Weavers as well as many others.

20

TV Programs Tonight On CBS:
7:30 To Tell the Truth
8:00 I've Got A Secret
8:30 The Lucy Show
9:00 Danny Thomas
9:30 Andy Griffith
10:00 The New Loretta Young Show
10:30 The Stars

21

"Little" Stevie Wonder records his second album, "The Twelve-Year-Old Genius", live at a Detroit ballroom. One song on the album "Fingertips, Part Two" will become Wonder's first hit, eventually topping both the pop and R & B charts.

From The Hit Parade:
The #1 pop single is "If You Wanna Be Happy" by Jimmy Soul.

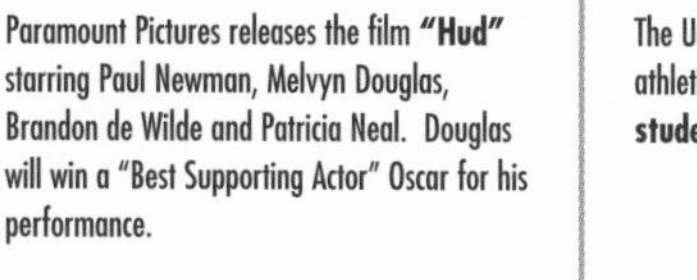

22

Dr. William Unsoeld, 36, and Dr. Thomas Hornbein, 32, are the first to climb **Mount Everest** via the treacherous West Ridge. James Whittaker, 32, was the first American to reach the summit May 1st. Barry Bishop, 30, and Luther Jerstad also reach the world's tallest peak, measured at 29,028 ft.

23

The United States **Postal Service** is charging customers 5¢ to mail a first-class letter anywhere within the U.S. The U.S. Post Office first began service in 1775, collecting a minimum of 6¢ to deliver a letter less than 30 miles up to a maximum of 25¢ for over 450 miles.

President Kennedy is selected as **Father Of The Year** by a National Committee.

24

Electric blues guitarist **Elmore James** suffers a fatal heart attack in Chicago at the age of 45. The Mississippi bluesman is one of the most influential guitarists, with followers including Johnny Winter, Eric Clapton, Keith Richards.

Attorney General Robert Kennedy meets Governor George Wallace in Alabama as part of a southern tour focusing on racial tensions.

25

Following a recent announcement that the **Dallas Texans**, 1962 winners of the American Football League championship, would be moving to Kansas City, owner Lamar Hunt proclaims that the team will be called the Chiefs for the upcoming season.

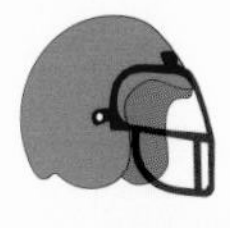

26

The annual television **Emmy Awards** include:
Best Program of the Year: "The Tunnel"
Best Comedy: "The Dick Van Dyke Show"
Best Variety: "The Andy Williams Show"
Best Children's Program: Walt Disney's "Wonderful World of Color"
Best Dramatic Program: "The Defenders"
Best Actress: Shirley Booth "Hazel"
Best Actor (Series): E.G. Marshall "The Defenders"

27

Morrow Publishing releases the novel **"The Shoes of the Fisherman"** by Morris L. West. The story of a Russian who becomes the Pope will become the best-selling nonfiction work for this year and will become the basis of a film starring Anthony Quinn in 1968.

28

Paramount Pictures releases the film **"Hud"** starring Paul Newman, Melvyn Douglas, Brandon de Wilde and Patricia Neal. Douglas will win a "Best Supporting Actor" Oscar for his performance.

29

The University of Kentucky announces that its athletic teams **"will now be open to any student regardless of race"**.

Bob Hope celebrates his 60th birthday.

President John F. Kennedy celebrates his 46th birthday.

30

The 47th **Indianapolis 500** Car Race is won by Parnelli Jones, 29, driving his Watson with a front engine Offy at a new average speed record of 143.137 mph. Jones sets a one-lap race record of 151.541 mph. Jim Clark, 27, of Scotland finishes 2nd, and A.J. Foyt of Houston places third. Jim Clark, who receives "Rookie of the Year" honors, will win the race in 1965.

31

A cyclone with winds of up to 162 mph has battered the coast of East Pakistan since May 28th, killing some 22,000 people.

Judy Audsley of Kansas City and **Dick Weber** of St. Louis win the Women's and Men's titles at the Bowling Tournament of Champions in N.Y.

Paul Newman and Melvyn Douglas in a scene from the new movie "Hud". (See May 28th)

Race car driver Parnelli Jones leaves the track after setting a new oval speed mark of 152.27 mph while qualifying for the Indy 500. (See also May 30th)

Folk musician Bob Dylan, 22, walks out during rehearsal for "The Ed Sullivan Show". (See May 12th)

Sean Connery stars in his first appearance as "James Bond" in the film "Dr. No".

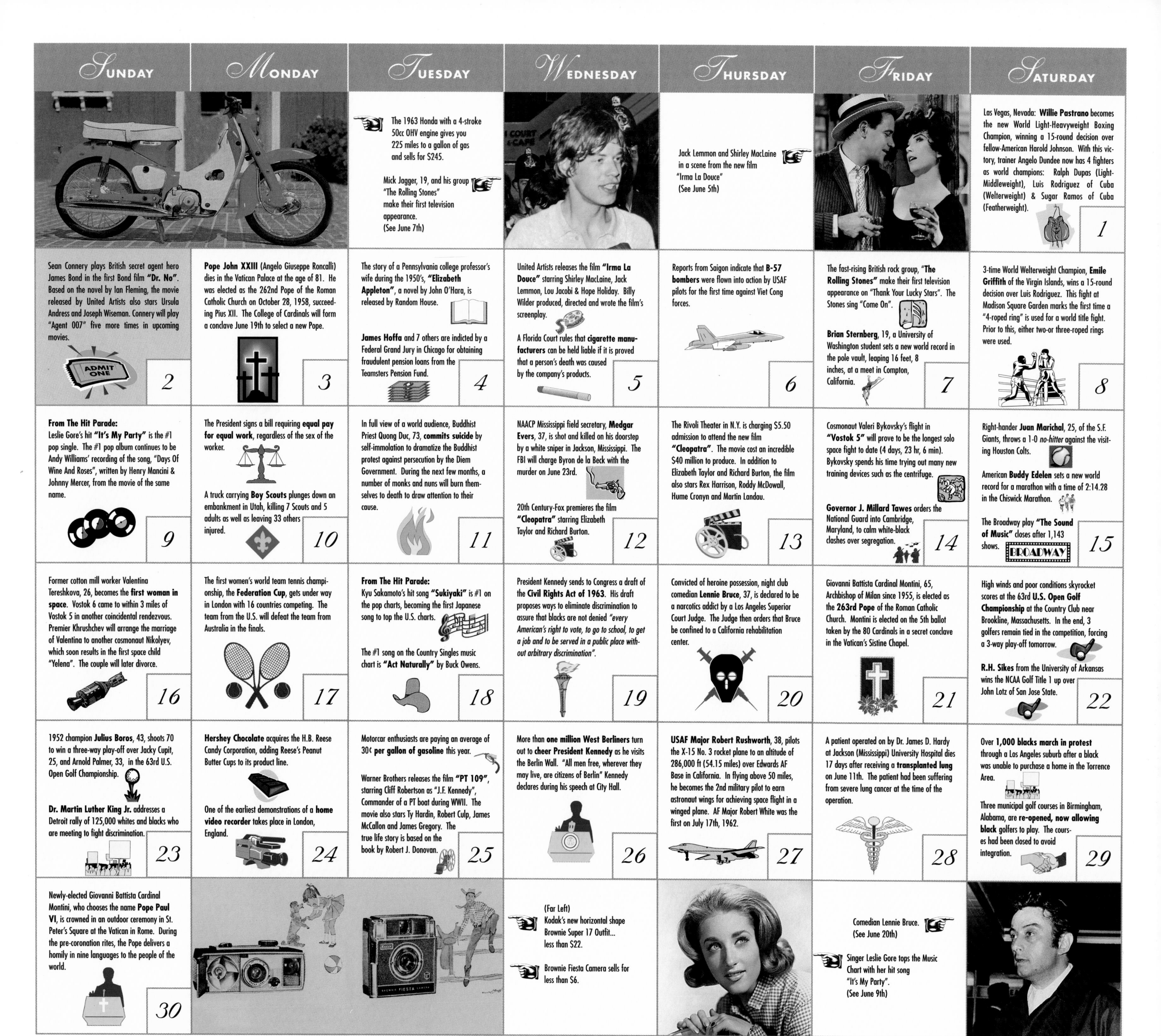

Sunday	Monday	Tuesday	Wednesday	Thursday	Friday	Saturday
		The 1963 Honda with a 4-stroke 50cc OHV engine gives you 225 miles to a gallon of gas and sells for $245. Mick Jagger, 19, and his group "The Rolling Stones" make their first television appearance. (See June 7th)		Jack Lemmon and Shirley MacLaine in a scene from the new film "Irma La Douce" (See June 5th)		Las Vegas, Nevada: **Willie Pastrano** becomes the new World Light-Heavyweight Boxing Champion, winning a 15-round decision over fellow-American Harold Johnson. With this victory, trainer Angelo Dundee now has 4 fighters as world champions: Ralph Dupas (Light-Middleweight), Luis Rodriguez of Cuba (Welterweight) & Sugar Ramos of Cuba (Featherweight). 1
Sean Connery plays British secret agent hero James Bond in the first Bond film **"Dr. No"**. Based on the novel by Ian Fleming, the movie released by United Artists also stars Ursula Andress and Joseph Wiseman. Connery will play "Agent 007" five more times in upcoming movies. ADMIT ONE 2	**Pope John XXIII** (Angelo Giuseppe Roncalli) dies in the Vatican Palace at the age of 81. He was elected as the 262nd Pope of the Roman Catholic Church on October 28, 1958, succeeding Pius XII. The College of Cardinals will form a conclave June 19th to select a new Pope. 3	The story of a Pennsylvania college professor's wife during the 1950's, **"Elizabeth Appleton"**, a novel by John O'Hara, is released by Random House. **James Hoffa** and 7 others are indicted by a Federal Grand Jury in Chicago for obtaining fraudulent pension loans from the Teamsters Pension Fund. 4	United Artists releases the film **"Irma La Douce"** starring Shirley MacLaine, Jack Lemmon, Lou Jacobi & Hope Holiday. Billy Wilder produced, directed and wrote the film's screenplay. A Florida Court rules that **cigarette manufacturers** can be held liable if it is proved that a person's death was caused by the company's products. 5	Reports from Saigon indicate that **B-57 bombers** were flown into action by USAF pilots for the first time against Viet Cong forces. 6	The fast-rising British rock group, **"The Rolling Stones"** make their first television appearance on "Thank Your Lucky Stars". The Stones sing "Come On". **Brian Sternberg**, 19, a University of Washington student sets a new world record in the pole vault, leaping 16 feet, 8 inches, at a meet in Compton, California. 7	3-time World Welterweight Champion, **Emile Griffith** of the Virgin Islands, wins a 15-round decision over Luis Rodriguez. This fight at Madison Square Garden marks the first time a "4-roped ring" is used for a world title fight. Prior to this, either two-or three-roped rings were used. 8
From The Hit Parade: Leslie Gore's hit **"It's My Party"** is the #1 pop single. The #1 pop album continues to be Andy Williams' recording of the song, "Days Of Wine And Roses", written by Henry Mancini & Johnny Mercer, from the movie of the same name. 9	The President signs a bill requiring **equal pay for equal work**, regardless of the sex of the worker. A truck carrying **Boy Scouts** plunges down an embankment in Utah, killing 7 Scouts and 5 adults as well as leaving 33 others injured. 10	In full view of a world audience, Buddhist Priest Quong Duc, 73, **commits suicide** by self-immolation to dramatize the Buddhist protest against persecution by the Diem Government. During the next few months, a number of monks and nuns will burn themselves to death to draw attention to their cause. 11	NAACP Mississippi field secretary, **Medgar Evers**, 37, is shot and killed on his doorstep by a white sniper in Jackson, Mississippi. The FBI will charge Byron de la Beck with the murder on June 23rd. 20th Century-Fox premieres the film **"Cleopatra"** starring Elizabeth Taylor and Richard Burton. 12	The Rivoli Theater in N.Y. is charging $5.50 admission to attend the new film **"Cleopatra"**. The movie cost an incredible $40 million to produce. In addition to Elizabeth Taylor and Richard Burton, the film also stars Rex Harrison, Roddy McDowall, Hume Cronyn and Martin Landau. 13	Cosmonaut Valeri Bykovsky's flight in **"Vostok 5"** will prove to be the longest solo space fight to date (4 days, 23 hr, 6 min). Bykovsky spends his time trying out many new training devices such as the centrifuge. **Governor J. Millard Tawes** orders the National Guard into Cambridge, Maryland, to calm white-black clashes over segregation. 14	Right-hander **Juan Marichal**, 25, of the S.F. Giants, throws a 1-0 *no-hitter* against the visiting Houston Colts. American **Buddy Edelen** sets a new world record for a marathon with a time of 2:14.28 in the Chiswick Marathon. The Broadway play **"The Sound of Music"** closes after 1,143 shows. BROADWAY 15
Former cotton mill worker Valentina Tereshkova, 26, becomes the **first woman in space**. Vostok 6 came to within 3 miles of Vostok 5 in another coincidental rendezvous. Premier Khrushchev will arrange the marriage of Valentina to another cosmonaut Nikolyev, which soon results in the first space child "Yelena". The couple will later divorce. 16	The first women's world team tennis championship, the **Federation Cup**, gets under way in London with 16 countries competing. The team from the U.S. will defeat the team from Australia in the finals. 17	**From The Hit Parade:** Kyu Sakamoto's hit song **"Sukiyaki"** is #1 on the pop charts, becoming the first Japanese song to top the U.S. charts. The #1 song on the Country Singles music chart is **"Act Naturally"** by Buck Owens. 18	President Kennedy sends to Congress a draft of the **Civil Rights Act of 1963**. His draft proposes ways to eliminate discrimination to assure that blacks are not denied *"every American's right to vote, to go to school, to get a job and to be served in a public place without arbitrary discrimination"*. 19	Convicted of heroine possession, night club comedian **Lennie Bruce**, 37, is declared to be a narcotics addict by a Los Angeles Superior Court Judge. The Judge then orders that Bruce be confined to a California rehabilitation center. 20	Giovanni Battista Cardinal Montini, 65, Archbishop of Milan since 1955, is elected as the **263rd Pope** of the Roman Catholic Church. Montini is elected on the 5th ballot taken by the 80 Cardinals in a secret conclave in the Vatican's Sistine Chapel. 21	High winds and poor conditions skyrocket scores at the 63rd **U.S. Open Golf Championship** at the Country Club near Brookline, Massachusetts. In the end, 3 golfers remain tied in the competition, forcing a 3-way play-off tomorrow. **R.H. Sikes** from the University of Arkansas wins the NCAA Golf Title 1 up over John Lotz of San Jose State. 22
1952 champion **Julius Boros**, 43, shoots 70 to win a three-way play-off over Jacky Cupit, 25, and Arnold Palmer, 33, in the 63rd U.S. Open Golf Championship. **Dr. Martin Luther King Jr.** addresses a Detroit rally of 125,000 whites and blacks who are meeting to fight discrimination. 23	**Hershey Chocolate** acquires the H.B. Reese Candy Corporation, adding Reese's Peanut Butter Cups to its product line. One of the earliest demonstrations of a **home video recorder** takes place in London, England. 24	Motorcar enthusiasts are paying an average of 30¢ **per gallon of gasoline** this year. Warner Brothers releases the film **"PT 109"**, starring Cliff Robertson as "J.F. Kennedy", Commander of a PT boat during WWII. The movie also stars Ty Hardin, Robert Culp, James McCallon and James Gregory. The true life story is based on the book by Robert J. Donovan. 25	More than **one million West Berliners** turn out to **cheer President Kennedy** as he visits the Berlin Wall. "All men free, wherever they may live, are citizens of Berlin" Kennedy declares during his speech at City Hall. 26	**USAF Major Robert Rushworth**, 38, pilots the X-15 No. 3 rocket plane to an altitude of 286,000 ft (54.15 miles) over Edwards AF Base in California. In flying above 50 miles, he becomes the 2nd military pilot to earn astronaut wings for achieving space flight in a winged plane. AF Major Robert White was the first on July 17th, 1962. 27	A patient operated on by Dr. James D. Hardy at Jackson (Mississippi) University Hospital dies 17 days after receiving a **transplanted lung** on June 11th. The patient had been suffering from severe lung cancer at the time of the operation. 28	Over **1,000 blacks march in protest** through a Los Angeles suburb after a black was unable to purchase a home in the Torrence Area. Three municipal golf courses in Birmingham, Alabama, are **re-opened, now allowing black** golfers to play. The courses had been closed to avoid integration. 29
Newly-elected Giovanni Battista Cardinal Montini, who chooses the name **Pope Paul VI**, is crowned in an outdoor ceremony in St. Peter's Square at the Vatican in Rome. During the pre-coronation rites, the Pope delivers a homily in nine languages to the people of the world. 30			(Far Left) Kodak's new horizontal shape Brownie Super 17 Outfit... less than $22. Brownie Fiesta Camera sells for less than $6.		Comedian Lennie Bruce. (See June 20th) Singer Leslie Gore tops the Music Chart with her hit song "It's My Party". (See June 9th)	

JULY 1963

President Kennedy meets with Pope Paul VI at the Vatican in Rome.

Sunday | Monday | Tuesday | Wednesday | Thursday | Friday | Saturday

1
The "Golden Bear" Jack Nicklaus, 23, wins his second golf major of the year capturing the PGA Championship in Texas.
(See July 21st)

Golfer **Arnold Palmer**, 33, defeats Tony Lema, 29, and Tommy Aaron, 26, to win the Cleveland Open. The win is worth $22,000 to Palmer.

2
President Kennedy is given a private audience with Pope Paul VI at the Vatican. They spend 40 minutes speaking alone together in the Pope's private library. Mr. Kennedy is only the third President to be received in papal audience. The others were Woodrow Wilson in 1919 and Dwight D. Eisenhower in 1959. Kennedy is the 1st Roman Catholic to be elected President of the United States.

3
President Kennedy returns to a racially-torn U.S. following a **foreign state visit** to West Germany, Berlin, Ireland, England and Italy in an effort to cement western unity. In West Berlin, the President addressed 150,000 people pledging that the U.S. would defend the city's freedom.

4
The nation celebrates its **187th birthday**.

Major League Baseball Standings:
National League: L.A. Dodgers are 1/2 game up on St. Louis
American League: NY Yankees hold a 4-game lead on Minnesota

5
James Meredith, the first black enrolled at the University of Mississippi, **receives a cool reception** after addressing the 54th annual NAACP Convention Meeting in Chicago. Meredith is perceived as a moderate and responds to critics that the Civil Rights Movement is being endangered by "intolerance and bigotry" by black leaders.

6
American Chuck McKinley captures the 77th **Wimbledon** Men's Singles Tennis Championship over Australia's **Fred Stolle** 9-7, 6-1, 6-4. Australian **Margaret Smith** will win the Women's title, defeating American Billy Jean King 6-3, 6-4.

7
From The Hit Parade:
Gerry and The Pacemakers' hit **"I Like It"** is the #1 pop single in the United Kingdom. It will be replaced next week by Frank Ifield's hit "I'm Confessin'".

Golfer **Shirley Englehorn**, 22, wins the Woman's Eastern Open in Sutton, Massachusetts, to take the $1,500 1st prize.

8
"Chateaugay" with jockey Braulio Baeza aboard wins the 95th **Belmont Stakes** Horse Race for 3-year-old horses at Aqueduct Race Track, N.Y., in a time of 2:30 1/5. Second place goes to "Candy Spots" with "Choker" finishing third in this historic race first run in 1867.

9
The 34th Annual **Major League Baseball All-Star game** is won by the National League 5-3 over the American League squad in Cleveland, led by Willie May's two runs and two stolen bases. AL leads the series 17-16-1.

President Kennedy meets with 300 leaders **representing 50 million women** at a White House meeting to ask them to support his "Rights" programs.

10
The N.Y. State Court of Appeals rules 4-3 that the book **"Tropic of Cancer"** by author Henry Miller is "flagrantly obscene" and "dirt for dirt's sake". The State Supreme Courts in Massachusetts, California and Wisconsin have ruled the book to be "not obscene".

11
The Defense Department has announced that armed forces reserves have all been **"integrated"** eliminating **"all-Negro"** units. There are still 10 southern states however who do not allow blacks in their National Guard units.

12
McDonald's Restaurants have replaced mascot "Speedee" with a new figure, **Ronald McDonald**. Just two years ago Ray Kroc bought all rights from Richard and Maurice McDonald for $2.7 million. He had met the pair in 1954 when he persuaded them to begin selling franchises of their hamburger restaurant.

13
Left-handed golfer Bob Charles of New Zealand captures the 92nd **British Open** Golf Championship by 9 strokes in an 18-hole play-off over American Phil Rodgers at the Royal Lytham Country Club in England.

Early Wynn, 43, of the AL Cleveland Indians wins his 300th game, a 7-4 win over the Athletics in Kansas City.

14
The Southern Regional Council reports that 92 out of every 100 blacks in 17 southern states now attend **segregated schools**.

France's **Jacques Anquetil** wins the gruelling 2,570-mile Tour de France Bicycle Race. Anquetic also won the event in 1957, 1961, and 1962.

15
The popular **McDonald's** Restaurant, which opened its first restaurant in Des Plaines, Illinois, in April 1955, introduces its new menu that includes a Filet-O-Fish sandwich in addition to the regular items already offered.

16
Representative **Carl Vinson**, 79, (Democrat, Georgia) sets a record for serving in the House longer than any other person (48 years, 8 months, 13 days) surpassing the previous record set by the late House Speaker Sam Rayburn of Texas.

17
Paramount Pictures releases the zany comedy film **"The Nutty Professor"** starring Jerry Lewis, Stella Stevens, Del Moore and Kathleen Freeman. Lewis, who co-wrote the screenplay with Bill Richmond, also directed the movie.

18
Comedienne **Red Skelton** celebrates his 50th birthday.

Swedish lawnmower manufacturer Karl Dahlman, inspired by the "Hovercraft", introduces a new mower he markets as the **"Flymo".** Requiring no wheels, the Flymo operates on a cushion of air.

19
Americans who invest their savings in local banks across the country this year will receive an average of **4.1% interest** on a regular savings account.

20
A total **eclipse of the Sun** is visible in Japan, Alaska, Canada, Maine and the North Atlantic. Scientists warn the public not to look directly at the eclipse.

F-1 driver Jim Clark of Great Britain wins the **British Grand Prix** driving a Lotus. Clark, who won last year, will go on to win this race 3 more times before he will die in a crash in 1968.

21
The "Golden Bear", Jack Nicklaus, 23, shoots a final round of 68 to win the 45th **PGA Golf Championship** by 2 strokes over Dave Ragan at the Dallas Athletic Golf Club in Texas. The PGA was first formed during 1916. Nicklaus earns $13,000 for his victory.

22
In a rematch for the World Heavyweight Boxing Title, **Sonny Liston**, 30, retains the title he won from Floyd Patterson in September 1962, as he knocks out Patterson once again in the first round of their scheduled 15-round fight in Las Vegas, Nevada.

23
Young girls are playing for hours with their **"Barbie Dolls"**. Since their introduction in the late 1950's, over 4 million have now been sold. Barbie Dolls that retail for $3.00 also require fashions that are being sold at the rate of 100,000 costumes per week.

24
The Cuban Government issues a decree **expropriating the U.S. Embassy building** in Havana, including all furniture and equipment. This seizure comes in retaliation to the U.S. action July 8th when the U.S. Treasury Department froze all Cuban assets ($33 million) under provisions of the "trading with the enemy act".

25
Representatives from the U.S., Great Britain and the U.S.S.R. draft a **treaty prohibiting nuclear weapons tests** in the "Earth's atmosphere", in "outer space", or "under water". The treaty will be ratified by the Senate September 24th and will take effect on October 10th.

26
An **earthquake** that measures 6.1 on the Richter Scale strikes the City of Skopje, Yugoslavia, killing an estimated 1,500 people.

American **John Pennel** sets a new World Pole Vault record, leaping 16 feet 8 3/4 inches at a meet in Poland.

27
From The Hit Parade:
The #1 pop single is "Surf City" by Jan and Dean replacing "Easier Said Than Done" by The Essex.

The #1 song on the Country Singles music chart is **"Ring of Fire"** by Johnny Cash.

28
Arnold Palmer ties with Jack Nicklaus and Julius Boros at the Western Open Golf Tournament in Chicago. Palmer will win the event in a play-off tomorrow to capture the $11,000 winner's purse.

29
The **U.S. Breweries Association** reports that a record 10,215,147 barrels of beer and ale were sold during the past month by U.S. breweries. It is the first time over 10 million barrels have been sold during a single month.

Golfer **Kathy Whitworth**, 23, wins the $12,500 Milwaukee Open to take the $1,200 1st-place prize money.

30
The **New York Mets** of the National League end their Major League record losing streak of 22 games on the road, by defeating the L.A. Dodgers 5-1 in Los Angeles.

Consumers purchasing a loaf of **white bread** are paying an average price of 22¢ at supermarkets across the nation.

31
Great Britain watches as the final chapter of a **scandal** involving former Secretary of State for War, John Profumo, concludes. The Macmillan Government, rocked by the scandal, witnesses the conviction of Dr. Stephen Ward for living off the earnings of prostitutes Christine Keeler and Marilyn Rice-Davies. Ward will commit suicide over the scandal.

Beer cans will never be the same! Thanks to new snap...and roll it off tabs.

Jerry Lewis and Stella Stevens star in the new film "The Nutty Professor".
(See July 17th)

AUGUST 1963

Civil Rights leader Dr. Martin Luther King Jr. delivers his historic "I Have A Dream...." speech.

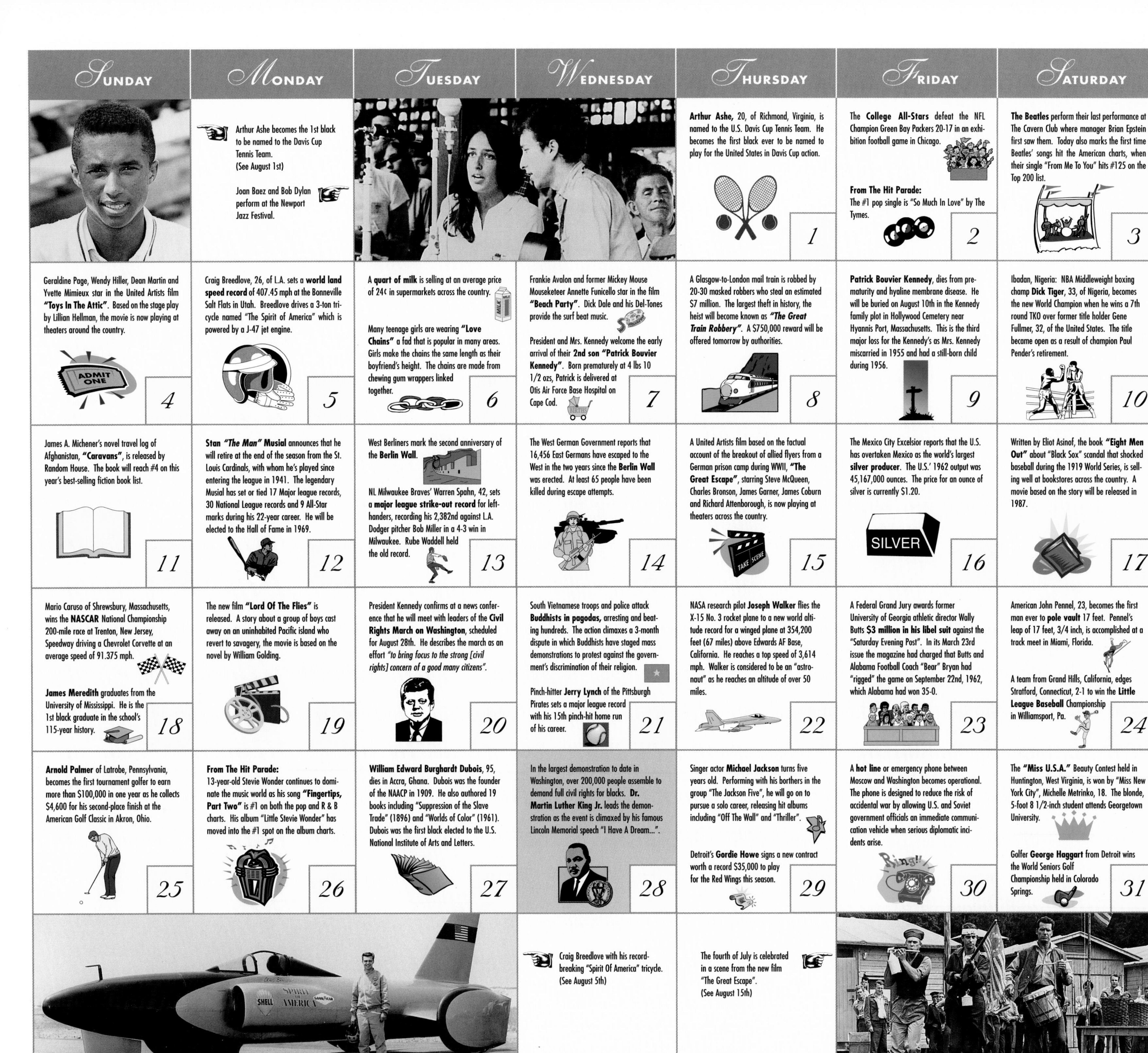

Sunday	Monday	Tuesday	Wednesday	Thursday	Friday	Saturday
	Arthur Ashe becomes the 1st black to be named to the Davis Cup Tennis Team. (See August 1st) Joan Baez and Bob Dylan perform at the Newport Jazz Festival.			**Arthur Ashe,** 20, of Richmond, Virginia, is named to the U.S. Davis Cup Tennis Team. He becomes the first black ever to be named to play for the United States in Davis Cup action. 1	The **College All-Stars** defeat the NFL Champion Green Bay Packers 20-17 in an exhibition football game in Chicago. **From The Hit Parade:** The #1 pop single is "So Much In Love" by The Tymes. 2	**The Beatles** perform their last performance at The Cavern Club where manager Brian Epstein first saw them. Today also marks the first time Beatles' songs hit the American charts, when their single "From Me To You" hits #125 on the Top 200 list. 3
Geraldine Page, Wendy Hiller, Dean Martin and Yvette Mimieux star in the United Artists film **"Toys In The Attic"**. Based on the stage play by Lillian Hellman, the movie is now playing at theaters around the country. 4	Craig Breedlove, 26, of L.A. sets a **world land speed record** of 407.45 mph at the Bonneville Salt Flats in Utah. Breedlove drives a 3-ton tricycle named "The Spirit of America" which is powered by a J-47 jet engine. 5	A **quart of milk** is selling at an average price of 24¢ in supermarkets across the country. Many teenage girls are wearing **"Love Chains"** a fad that is popular in many areas. Girls make the chains the same length as their boyfriend's height. The chains are made from chewing gum wrappers linked together. 6	Frankie Avalon and former Mickey Mouse Mouseketeer Annette Funicello star in the film **"Beach Party"**. Dick Dale and his Del-Tones provide the surf beat music. President and Mrs. Kennedy welcome the early arrival of their **2nd son "Patrick Bouvier Kennedy"**. Born prematurely at 4 lbs 10 1/2 ozs, Patrick is delivered at Otis Air Force Base Hospital on Cape Cod. 7	A Glasgow-to-London mail train is robbed by 20-30 masked robbers who steal an estimated $7 million. The largest theft in history, the heist will become known as ***"The Great Train Robbery"***. A $750,000 reward will be offered tomorrow by authorities. 8	**Patrick Bouvier Kennedy**, dies from prematurity and hyaline membrane disease. He will be buried on August 10th in the Kennedy family plot in Hollywood Cemetery near Hyannis Port, Massachusetts. This is the third major loss for the Kennedy's as Mrs. Kennedy miscarried in 1955 and had a still-born child during 1956. 9	Ibadan, Nigeria: NBA Middleweight boxing champ **Dick Tiger**, 33, of Nigeria, becomes the new World Champion when he wins a 7th round TKO over former title holder Gene Fullmer, 32, of the United States. The title became open as a result of champion Paul Pender's retirement. 10
James A. Michener's novel travel log of Afghanistan, **"Caravans"**, is released by Random House. The book will reach #4 on this year's best-selling fiction book list. 11	**Stan *"The Man"* Musial** announces that he will retire at the end of the season from the St. Louis Cardinals, with whom he's played since entering the league in 1941. The legendary Musial has set or tied 17 Major league records, 30 National League records and 9 All-Star marks during his 22-year career. He will be elected to the Hall of Fame in 1969. 12	West Berliners mark the second anniversary of the **Berlin Wall**. NL Milwaukee Braves' Warren Spahn, 42, sets a **major league strike-out record** for left-handers, recording his 2,382nd against L.A. Dodger pitcher Bob Miller in a 4-3 win in Milwaukee. Rube Waddell held the old record. 13	The West German Government reports that 16,456 East Germans have escaped to the West in the two years since the **Berlin Wall** was erected. At least 65 people have been killed during escape attempts. 14	A United Artists film based on the factual account of the breakout of allied flyers from a German prison camp during WWII, **"The Great Escape"**, starring Steve McQueen, Charles Bronson, James Garner, James Coburn and Richard Attenborough, is now playing at theaters across the country. 15	The Mexico City Excelsior reports that the U.S. has overtaken Mexico as the world's largest **silver producer**. The U.S.' 1962 output was 45,167,000 ounces. The price for an ounce of silver is currently $1.20. 16	Written by Eliot Asinof, the book **"Eight Men Out"** about "Black Sox" scandal that shocked baseball during the 1919 World Series, is selling well at bookstores across the country. A movie based on the story will be released in 1987. 17
Mario Caruso of Shrewsbury, Massachusetts, wins the **NASCAR** National Championship 200-mile race at Trenton, New Jersey, Speedway driving a Chevrolet Corvette at an average speed of 91.375 mph. **James Meredith** graduates from the University of Mississippi. He is the 1st black graduate in the school's 115-year history. 18	The new film **"Lord Of The Flies"** is released. A story about a group of boys cast away on an uninhabited Pacific island who revert to savagery, the movie is based on the novel by William Golding. 19	President Kennedy confirms at a news conference that he will meet with leaders of the **Civil Rights March on Washington**, scheduled for August 28th. He describes the march as an effort *"to bring focus to the strong [civil rights] concern of a good many citizens"*. 20	South Vietnamese troops and police attack **Buddhists in pagodas,** arresting and beating hundreds. The action climaxes a 3-month dispute in which Buddhists have staged mass demonstrations to protest against the government's discrimination of their religion. Pinch-hitter **Jerry Lynch** of the Pittsburgh Pirates sets a major league record with his 15th pinch-hit home run of his career. 21	NASA research pilot **Joseph Walker** flies the X-15 No. 3 rocket plane to a new world altitude record for a winged plane at 354,200 feet (67 miles) above Edwards AF Base, California. He reaches a top speed of 3,614 mph. Walker is considered to be an "astronaut" as he reaches an altitude of over 50 miles. 22	A Federal Grand Jury awards former University of Georgia athletic director Wally Butts **$3 million in his libel suit** against the "Saturday Evening Post". In its March 23rd issue the magazine had charged that Butts and Alabama Football Coach "Bear" Bryan had "rigged" the game on September 22nd, 1962, which Alabama had won 35-0. 23	American John Pennel, 23, becomes the first man ever to **pole vault** 17 feet. Pennel's leap of 17 feet, 3/4 inch, is accomplished at a track meet in Miami, Florida. A team from Grand Hills, California, edges Stratford, Connecticut, 2-1 to win the **Little League Baseball** Championship in Williamsport, Pa. 24
Arnold Palmer of Latrobe, Pennsylvania, becomes the first tournament golfer to earn more than $100,000 in one year as he collects $4,600 for his second-place finish at the American Golf Classic in Akron, Ohio. 25	**From The Hit Parade:** 13-year-old Stevie Wonder continues to dominate the music world as his song **"Fingertips, Part Two"** is #1 on both the pop and R & B charts. His album "Little Stevie Wonder" has moved into the #1 spot on the album charts. 26	**William Edward Burghardt Dubois**, 95, dies in Accra, Ghana. Dubois was the founder of the NAACP in 1909. He also authored 19 books including "Suppression of the Slave Trade" (1896) and "Worlds of Color" (1961). Dubois was the first black elected to the U.S. National Institute of Arts and Letters. 27	In the largest demonstration to date in Washington, over 200,000 people assemble to demand full civil rights for blacks. **Dr. Martin Luther King Jr.** leads the demonstration as the event is climaxed by his famous Lincoln Memorial speech "I Have A Dream...". 28	Singer actor **Michael Jackson** turns five years old. Performing with his borthers in the group "The Jackson Five", he will go on to pursue a solo career, releasing hit albums including "Off The Wall" and "Thriller". Detroit's **Gordie Howe** signs a new contract worth a record $35,000 to play for the Red Wings this season. 29	A **hot line** or emergency phone between Moscow and Washington becomes operational. The phone is designed to reduce the risk of accidental war by allowing U.S. and Soviet government officials an immediate communication vehicle when serious diplomatic incidents arise. 30	The **"Miss U.S.A."** Beauty Contest held in Huntington, West Virginia, is won by "Miss New York City", Michelle Metrinko, 18. The blonde, 5-foot 8 1/2-inch student attends Georgetown University. Golfer **George Haggart** from Detroit wins the World Seniors Golf Championship held in Colorado Springs. 31
			Craig Breedlove with his record-breaking "Spirit Of America" tricycle. (See August 5th)	The fourth of July is celebrated in a scene from the new film "The Great Escape". (See August 15th)		

SEPTEMBER 1963

David Janssen stars as "Dr. Richard Kimble" on the run in the new TV drama series "The Fugitive".

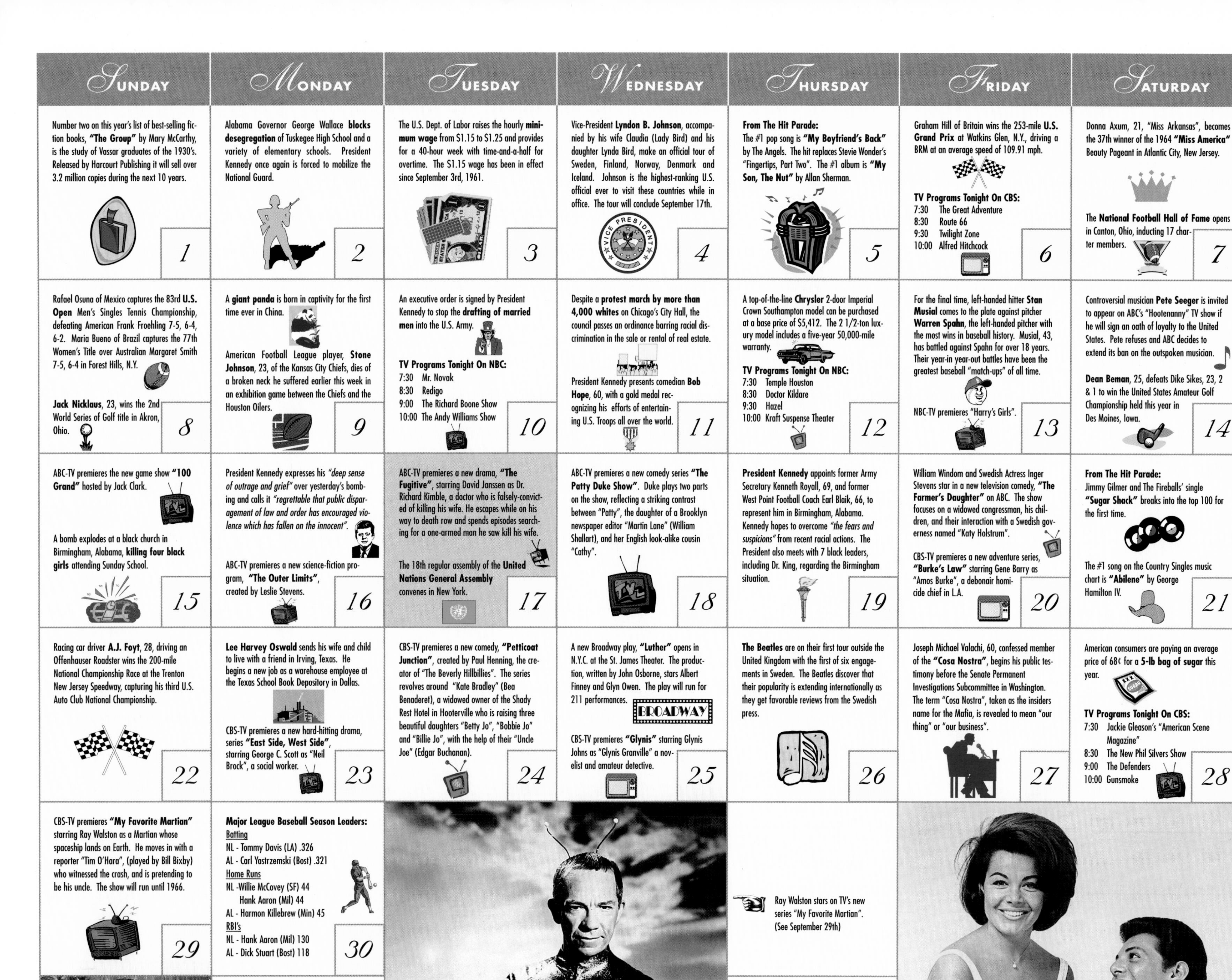

Sunday | Monday | Tuesday | Wednesday | Thursday | Friday | Saturday

1
Number two on this year's list of best-selling fiction books, **"The Group"** by Mary McCarthy, is the study of Vassar graduates of the 1930's. Released by Harcourt Publishing it will sell over 3.2 million copies during the next 10 years.

2
Alabama Governor George Wallace **blocks desegregation** of Tuskegee High School and a variety of elementary schools. President Kennedy once again is forced to mobilize the National Guard.

3
The U.S. Dept. of Labor raises the hourly **minimum wage** from $1.15 to $1.25 and provides for a 40-hour week with time-and-a-half for overtime. The $1.15 wage has been in effect since September 3rd, 1961.

4
Vice-President **Lyndon B. Johnson**, accompanied by his wife Claudia (Lady Bird) and his daughter Lynda Bird, make an official tour of Sweden, Finland, Norway, Denmark and Iceland. Johnson is the highest-ranking U.S. official ever to visit these countries while in office. The tour will conclude September 17th.

5
From The Hit Parade:
The #1 pop song is **"My Boyfriend's Back"** by The Angels. The hit replaces Stevie Wonder's "Fingertips, Part Two". The #1 album is **"My Son, The Nut"** by Allan Sherman.

6
Graham Hill of Britain wins the 253-mile **U.S. Grand Prix** at Watkins Glen, N.Y., driving a BRM at an average speed of 109.91 mph.

TV Programs Tonight On CBS:
7:30 The Great Adventure
8:30 Route 66
9:30 Twilight Zone
10:00 Alfred Hitchcock

7
Donna Axum, 21, "Miss Arkansas", becomes the 37th winner of the 1964 **"Miss America"** Beauty Pageant in Atlantic City, New Jersey.

The **National Football Hall of Fame** opens in Canton, Ohio, inducting 17 charter members.

8
Rafael Osuna of Mexico captures the 83rd **U.S. Open** Men's Singles Tennis Championship, defeating American Frank Froehling 7-5, 6-4, 6-2. Maria Bueno of Brazil captures the 77th Women's Title over Australian Margaret Smith 7-5, 6-4 in Forest Hills, N.Y.

Jack Nicklaus, 23, wins the 2nd World Series of Golf title in Akron, Ohio.

9
A **giant panda** is born in captivity for the first time ever in China.

American Football League player, **Stone Johnson**, 23, of the Kansas City Chiefs, dies of a broken neck he suffered earlier this week in an exhibition game between the Chiefs and the Houston Oilers.

10
An executive order is signed by President Kennedy to stop the **drafting of married men** into the U.S. Army.

TV Programs Tonight On NBC:
7:30 Mr. Novak
8:30 Redigo
9:00 The Richard Boone Show
10:00 The Andy Williams Show

11
Despite a **protest march by more than 4,000 whites** on Chicago's City Hall, the council passes an ordinance barring racial discrimination in the sale or rental of real estate.

President Kennedy presents comedian **Bob Hope**, 60, with a gold medal recognizing his efforts of entertaining U.S. Troops all over the world.

12
A top-of-the-line **Chrysler** 2-door Imperial Crown Southampton model can be purchased at a base price of $5,412. The 2 1/2-ton luxury model includes a five-year 50,000-mile warranty.

TV Programs Tonight On NBC:
7:30 Temple Houston
8:30 Doctor Kildare
9:30 Hazel
10:00 Kraft Suspense Theater

13
For the final time, left-handed hitter **Stan Musial** comes to the plate against pitcher **Warren Spahn**, the left-handed pitcher with the most wins in baseball history. Musial, 43, has battled against Spahn for over 18 years. Their year-in year-out battles have been the greatest baseball "match-ups" of all time.

NBC-TV premieres "Harry's Girls".

14
Controversial musician **Pete Seeger** is invited to appear on ABC's "Hootenanny" TV show if he will sign an oath of loyalty to the United States. Pete refuses and ABC decides to extend its ban on the outspoken musician.

Dean Beman, 25, defeats Dike Sikes, 23, 2 & 1 to win the United States Amateur Golf Championship held this year in Des Moines, Iowa.

15
ABC-TV premieres the new game show **"100 Grand"** hosted by Jack Clark.

A bomb explodes at a black church in Birmingham, Alabama, **killing four black girls** attending Sunday School.

16
President Kennedy expresses his *"deep sense of outrage and grief"* over yesterday's bombing and calls it *"regrettable that public disparagement of law and order has encouraged violence which has fallen on the innocent"*.

ABC-TV premieres a new science-fiction program, **"The Outer Limits"**, created by Leslie Stevens.

17
ABC-TV premieres a new drama, **"The Fugitive"**, starring David Janssen as Dr. Richard Kimble, a doctor who is falsely-convicted of killing his wife. He escapes while on his way to death row and spends episodes searching for a one-armed man he saw kill his wife.

The 18th regular assembly of the **United Nations General Assembly** convenes in New York.

18
ABC-TV premieres a new comedy series **"The Patty Duke Show"**. Duke plays two parts on the show, reflecting a striking contrast between "Patty", the daughter of a Brooklyn newspaper editor "Martin Lane" (William Shallart), and her English look-alike cousin "Cathy".

19
President Kennedy appoints former Army Secretary Kenneth Royall, 69, and former West Point Football Coach Earl Blaik, 66, to represent him in Birmingham, Alabama. Kennedy hopes to overcome *"the fears and suspicions"* from recent racial actions. The President also meets with 7 black leaders, including Dr. King, regarding the Birmingham situation.

20
William Windom and Swedish Actress Inger Stevens star in a new television comedy, **"The Farmer's Daughter"** on ABC. The show focuses on a widowed congressman, his children, and their interaction with a Swedish governess named "Katy Holstrum".

CBS-TV premieres a new adventure series, **"Burke's Law"** starring Gene Barry as "Amos Burke", a debonair homicide chief in L.A.

21
From The Hit Parade:
Jimmy Gilmer and The Fireballs' single **"Sugar Shack"** breaks into the top 100 for the first time.

The #1 song on the Country Singles music chart is **"Abilene"** by George Hamilton IV.

22
Racing car driver **A.J. Foyt**, 28, driving an Offenhauser Roadster wins the 200-mile National Championship Race at the Trenton New Jersey Speedway, capturing his third U.S. Auto Club National Championship.

23
Lee Harvey Oswald sends his wife and child to live with a friend in Irving, Texas. He begins a new job as a warehouse employee at the Texas School Book Depository in Dallas.

CBS-TV premieres a new hard-hitting drama, series **"East Side, West Side"**, starring George C. Scott as "Neil Brock", a social worker.

24
CBS-TV premieres a new comedy, **"Petticoat Junction"**, created by Paul Henning, the creator of "The Beverly Hillbillies". The series revolves around "Kate Bradley" (Bea Benaderet), a widowed owner of the Shady Rest Hotel in Hooterville who is raising three beautiful daughters "Betty Jo", "Bobbie Jo" and "Billie Jo", with the help of their "Uncle Joe" (Edgar Buchanan).

25
A new Broadway play, **"Luther"** opens in N.Y.C. at the St. James Theater. The production, written by John Osborne, stars Albert Finney and Glyn Owen. The play will run for 211 performances.

CBS-TV premieres **"Glynis"** starring Glynis Johns as "Glynis Granville" a novelist and amateur detective.

26
The Beatles are on their first tour outside the United Kingdom with the first of six engagements in Sweden. The Beatles discover that their popularity is extending internationally as they get favorable reviews from the Swedish press.

27
Joseph Michael Valachi, 60, confessed member of the **"Cosa Nostra"**, begins his public testimony before the Senate Permanent Investigations Subcommittee in Washington. The term "Cosa Nostra", taken as the insiders name for the Mafia, is revealed to mean "our thing" or "our business".

28
American consumers are paying an average price of 68¢ for a **5-lb bag of sugar** this year.

TV Programs Tonight On CBS:
7:30 Jackie Gleason's "American Scene Magazine"
8:30 The New Phil Silvers Show
9:00 The Defenders
10:00 Gunsmoke

29
CBS-TV premieres **"My Favorite Martian"** starring Ray Walston as a Martian whose spaceship lands on Earth. He moves in with a reporter "Tim O'Hara", (played by Bill Bixby) who witnessed the crash, and is pretending to be his uncle. The show will run until 1966.

30
Major League Baseball Season Leaders:
Batting
NL - Tommy Davis (LA) .326
AL - Carl Yastrzemski (Bost) .321
Home Runs
NL - Willie McCovey (SF) 44
Hank Aaron (Mil) 44
AL - Harmon Killebrew (Min) 45
RBI's
NL - Hank Aaron (Mil) 130
AL - Dick Stuart (Bost) 118

Ray Walston stars on TV's new series "My Favorite Martian". (See September 29th)

The new "Miss America", Donna Axum "Miss Alabama". (See September 7th)

Annette Funicello and Frankie Avalon star in the film "Beach Party". (See August 7th)

OCTOBER *1963*

Los Angeles Dodgers - 1963 World Series Champions

Sunday	Monday	Tuesday	Wednesday	Thursday	Friday	Saturday

1 (Tuesday)
Sidney Poitier is a jack-of-all trades who builds a chapel for five East German refugee nuns on the edge of the Arizona desert in the United Artists' release of the film **"Lilies of the Field"**. Poitier becomes the first black to win an Oscar for "Best Actor" for his performance.

2 (Wednesday)
The visiting National League champion **L.A. Dodgers** defeat the American League and two-time defending world champion NY Yankees 5-2 in game one of the 60th Annual World Series of Baseball. Sandy Koufax, 27, strikes out 15 Yankees to set a new world series record.

3 (Thursday)
The visiting **L.A. Dodgers** on 10 hits defeat the Yankees 4-1, led by Willie Davis who doubles in the 1st to score two runs, then scores himself in the 8th after reaching base on his second double of the game. Bill Skowron homered in the 4th as Pitcher Johnny Podres records the win.

President Kennedy attends the dedication of **"Greer's Ferry Dam"** in Arkansas.

4 (Friday)
Alistair MacLean's adventure novel about the Arctic **"Ice Station Zebra"** is released by Doubleday.

TV Programs Tonight On ABC:
7:30 77 Sunset Strip
8:30 Burke's Law
9:30 The Farmer's Daughter
10:00 Fight of the Week

5 (Saturday)
The **NHL 17th Annual All-Star game** is played in Toronto with the defending Stanley Cup champs, the Toronto Maple Leafs, against the league's best. They play to a 3-3 tie with Frank Mahovlich scoring 2 goals for Toronto.

The home-field L.A. Dodgers make it **3 games in a row** with a 1-0 win. Pitcher Don Drysdale goes the distance, allowing just 3 hits to record the win.

6 (Sunday)
Dodger **Joe Pepitone** scores the winning run from third on an outfield fly by Willie Davis in the 7th inning to give L.A. a 2-1 win and a 4-game sweep of the Yankees to win the World Series of Baseball. Koufax gets his second win of the series and wins the MVP. Managed by Walt Alston, L.A. hit for a combined low 2.14 avg but had a composite pitching ERA of just 1.00.

7 (Monday)
Hurricane Flora, that has been ravaging the Caribbean for the last 3 days, has caused 6,000 deaths, mostly in Haiti.

TV Programs Tonight On CBS:
8:00 I've Got A Secret
8:30 The Lucy Show
9:00 Danny Thomas
9:30 Andy Griffith

8 (Tuesday)
Two U.S. Marine **helicopters crash** in the Da Nang Area, 350 miles north of Saigon, killing all 12 Americans on board. U.S. officials will report that, since January 1st, 1961, 60 Americans have now been killed during combat in Vietnam. This report comes a week after the White House announced that the U.S. will continue giving support to South Vietnam and that its major task should be completed by the end of 1965.

9 (Wednesday)
A major **flood** occurs in northern Italy as a wave crashes over the 873-ft-high Vaiont Dam (the world's 3rd highest) killing over 1,800 people. The alpine village of Longarone is virtually destroyed along with several other communities. U.S. helicopters aid in rescue operations.

President Kennedy authorizes the sale of **$250 million** worth of wheat to the U.S.S.R.

10 (Thursday)
British Prime Minister **Harold MacMillan**, 69, announces his plans to retire after 7 years in office, citing poor health. His resignation will be effective October 18th, with former Foreign Secretary Lord Alec Douglas-Home succeeding MacMillan as Prime Minister.

A bill is passed authorizing $5.1 billion for NASA programs but bars any joint manned flights to the moon with any Communist power.

11 (Friday)
From The Hit Parade:
The #1 pop single is **"Sugar Shack"** by Jimmy Gilmer and The Fireballs, which replaces Bobby Vinton's hit "Blue Velvet".

The #1 song on the Country Singles Music Chart is **"Talk Back, Trembling Lips"** by Ernest Ashworth.

12 (Saturday)
The film adaptation of Henry Fielding's 18th-century novel **"Tom Jones"**, directed by Tony Richardson, starring Albert Finney, Susannah York, Hugh Griffith and Dame Edith Evans, is released by Lobert Pictures. The movie will win an Oscar for "Best Film".

13 (Sunday)
The U.S, led by captain Arnold Palmer, defeats Great Britain 23-9 to win the 15th Biennial **Ryder Cup Golf Challenge** at the Atlanta Golf Course. The U.S. now leads 12-3 in the series that first started in 1927.

The Beatles appear on the BBC's **"Sunday Night at the London Palladium"** TV show in England. The show is watched by over 15 million viewers.

14 (Monday)
It is estimated that the **world population** now stands at 3.2 billion people. It is also estimated that 56% of this total comes from Asia. The country with the largest population is China with 731 million. The U.S. now exceeds 190 million people with over 4 million new births during 1962 alone.

15 (Tuesday)
Men's World Tennis Rankings:
1) Rafael Osuna of Mexico
2) Charles McKinley of the U.S.A.
3) Roy Emerson of Australia

Women's World Tennis Rankings:
1) Margaret Smith from Australia (for the second straight year)
2) Lesley Turner of Australia
3) Maria Ester Bueno of Brazil

16 (Wednesday)
The nation's second-highest circulation newspaper (882,000), The **"New York Daily Mirror"**, ceases publication citing rising costs and the recent newspaper strike.

TV Programs Tonight On CBS:
8:30 Glynis
9:00 The Beverly Hillbillies
9:30 Dick Van Dyke
10:00 The Danny Kaye Show

17 (Thursday)
The **United Nations General Assembly** adopts a new resolution calling on all nations to refrain from placing **"nuclear arms in space"**. It received the unanimous approval of all 111 members of the assembly.

18 (Friday)
NASA announces its selection of 14 more jet pilots to be trained as **astronauts**, bringing the total to 30. The group includes the first astronaut with a doctorate, AF Major Edwin E. "Buzz" Aldrin Jr., 33.

The International **Olympic Committee selects Mexico City** as the site for the 1968 summer Olympics.

19 (Saturday)
President Kennedy is awarded an **honorary LLD Degree at the University of Maine**. Defending recent actions, Kennedy says there is nothing inconsistent with selling surplus wheat to the Russians while refusing to sell strategic items. Following his speech, the President visits the grave of his infant son Patrick Bouvier in Brookline, Mass.

20 (Sunday)
Fullback **Jim Brown** of the Cleveland Browns sets a new NFL career rushing record of 8,390 yards, as he gains 144 yards in a 37-7 victory over the Philadelphia Eagles.

Jack Nicklaus wins the $70,000 Sahara Invitational Event in Las Vegas taking home $13,000.

21 (Monday)
Cuban Premier Castro calls for *"an end to the [U.S.] economic blockade of our country, especially at this moment"*, referring to the present damage to Cuba suffered by Hurricane Flora. The U.S. State Dept. will reply on Oct. 23rd that it will *"maintain [its] present economic isolation of Cuba as long as the Cuban Government chooses to follow ...(an) aggressive course of hostility"* toward the United States.

22 (Tuesday)
The **Chrysler Motor Car Co.**, the 11th-largest producer of cars in the U.S., continues to sell their Newport model as its top model. 50% of its 11,000-car production are Newports, its least expensive car, based at $2,964.

The #1 hit on the Country Singles Chart is **"Love's Gonna Live Here"** by Buck Owens.

23 (Wednesday)
The Neil Simon comedy, **"Barefoot In The Park"**, opens on Broadway at the Biltmore Theatre in N.Y. Staged by Mike Nichols, the play stars Elizabeth Ashley and Robert Redford in his first starring role. Mike Nichols will win a Tony Award for "Best Director". The play will run for 1,530 performances.

BROADWAY

24 (Thursday)
Over the past 2 1/2 days, the entire U.S. 2nd Armored Division and its supporting units were airlifted from Ft. Hood, Texas, to air bases near Frankfurt, W. Germany, in a widely-publicized demonstration of the U.S.' ability to quickly commit a **large group to combat**.

Yogi Berra, 38, is named as manager of the NY Yankees at $35,000 a year.

25 (Friday)
Soviet Premier Khrushchev makes a statement saying that the U.S.S.R. is not racing the U.S. to get a man on the Moon. "At the present time we do not plan flights of cosmonauts to the moon". I have read "that Americans wish to land a man on the moon by 1970; well let's wish them success".

26 (Saturday)
Francis Gary Powers, 34, who was shot down during 1960 as pilot of a United States U-2 reconnaissance plane, marries Claudia Edwards Downey, 28, a Central Intelligence Agency psychologist. Powers' spy flight in 1960 became an international incident. Later, he was exchanged by the Soviets for spy Rudolf Abel during February, 1962.

27 (Sunday)
Formula 1 driver Jim Clark of Great Britain, driving a Lotus, wins the inaugural **Mexican Grand Prix** car race run in Mexico City at 7300 ft above sea level, the highest circuit run ever used for championship racing.

Golfer **Sandra Haynie**, 20, takes home $1,350 in winning the Thunderbird Women's Open in Phoenix, Arizona.

28 (Monday)
The 11th Annual **World Cup of Golf,** this year held at the Saint Nom-La-Breteche Golf Club in Versailles, France, is won by the United States for the 4th consecutive year. Representing the U.S. at the International event is Jack Nicklaus and Arnold Palmer.

29 (Tuesday)
The **Cy Young Memorial Award,** presented annually to Major League Baseball's best pitcher, goes to L.A. Dodger left-hander **Sandy Koufax**, 27, who won 25 while losing just 5 games with a sensational 1.88 ERA during this season.

30 (Wednesday)
Walt Disney releases the film **"The Incredible Journey"**. Based on the book by Sheila Burnford, the movie follows the 250-mile adventure of a cat "Tao" and two dogs "Bodger" and "Luath", as they journey home to be reunited with their owners.

31 (Thursday)
A tragic **gas explosion** rips through the Indianapolis State Fair Grounds Coliseum during a performance of the Holiday On Ice troupe. Caused by cooking gas escaping from a food concession, the blast kills 73 and injures an additional 330 spectators.

Lilia Skala and Sidney Poitier star in the new film "Lilies Of The Field". (See October 1st)

The Beatles appear on television in the U.K. (See October 13th)

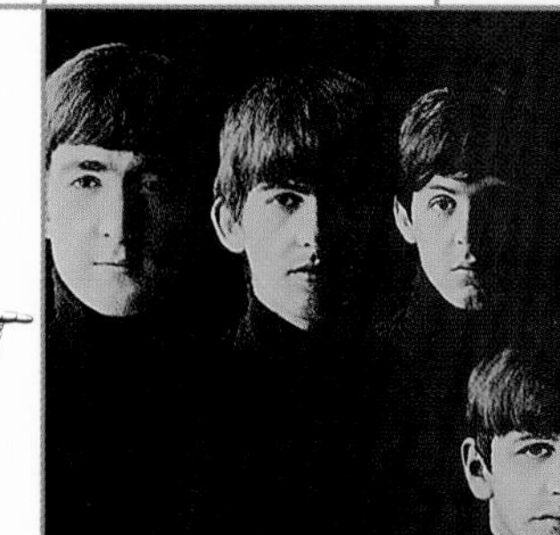

Albert Finney and Susannah York in a scene from the new film "Tom Jones". (See October 12th)

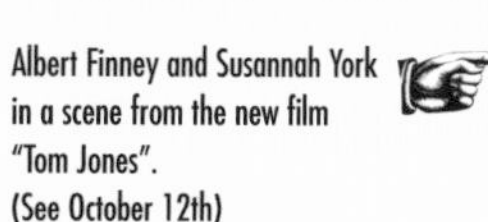

NOVEMBER 1963

President John F. Kennedy with wife Jacqueline wave to the crowd just moments before his assassination.

Sunday | Monday | Tuesday | Wednesday | Thursday | Friday | Saturday

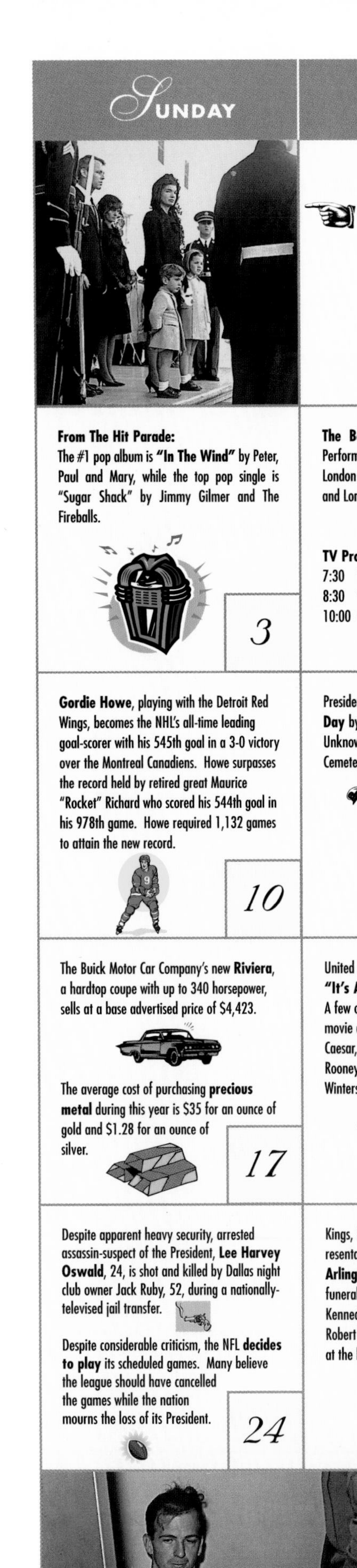

Mrs. Jacqueline Kennedy with children John Jr. and Caroline wait at the White House entrance for the late President's procession on November 24th.

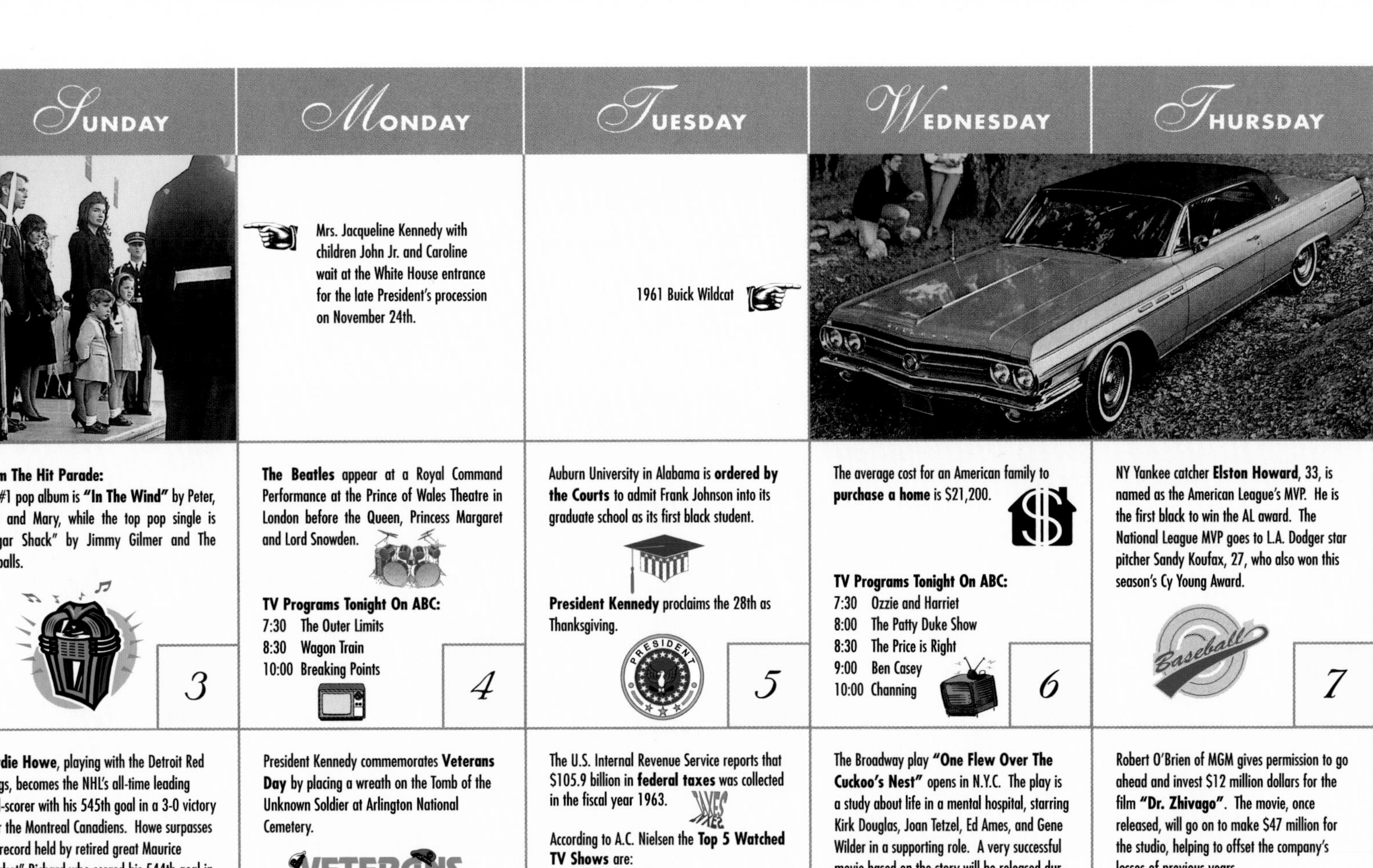

1961 Buick Wildcat

1

In a violent **coup d'etat**, South Vietnamese army troops oust President Na Dinh Diem and his brother Ngo Dinh Nhu, head of the Secret police. President Kennedy orders the 7th Fleet toward the area of South Vietnam to protect the 3,500 civilians and 16,500 military personnel "who might be" endangered as a result of the coup.

2

Ousted South Vietnamese President Na Dinh Diem and his brother are found dead. Some reports say they committed suicide while others report they were assassinated. A civilian-military government will assume office on November 4th, headed by Buddhist former-Vice-President Nguyen Ngoc Tho.

3

From The Hit Parade:
The #1 pop album is **"In The Wind"** by Peter, Paul and Mary, while the top pop single is "Sugar Shack" by Jimmy Gilmer and The Fireballs.

4

The Beatles appear at a Royal Command Performance at the Prince of Wales Theatre in London before the Queen, Princess Margaret and Lord Snowden.

TV Programs Tonight On ABC:
7:30 The Outer Limits
8:30 Wagon Train
10:00 Breaking Points

5

Auburn University in Alabama is **ordered by the Courts** to admit Frank Johnson into its graduate school as its first black student.

President Kennedy proclaims the 28th as Thanksgiving.

6

The average cost for an American family to **purchase a home** is $21,200.

TV Programs Tonight On ABC:
7:30 Ozzie and Harriet
8:00 The Patty Duke Show
8:30 The Price is Right
9:00 Ben Casey
10:00 Channing

7

NY Yankee catcher **Elston Howard**, 33, is named as the American League's MVP. He is the first black to win the AL award. The National League MVP goes to L.A. Dodger star pitcher Sandy Koufax, 27, who also won this season's Cy Young Award.

8

Dick Clark's **"Caravan of Stars"**, a live music show, opens in New Jersey including Bobby Vee, Brian Hyland, The Ronettes, Little Eva and many more.

The Dutch firm **Phillips** introduces the first true **compact cassette, the C-60** which allows 30 minutes playing time per side. The first cassettes are blank but will become the new way to replay music, replacing 8-track tapes.

9

The Baseball Writer's Association announces that 2nd-baseman Pete Rose, 22, of the Cincinnati Reds and pitcher Gary Peters, 26, of the Chicago White Sox, as the National and American League **"Rookies of The Year"** in Major League Baseball.

10

Gordie Howe, playing with the Detroit Red Wings, becomes the NHL's all-time leading goal-scorer with his 545th goal in a 3-0 victory over the Montreal Canadiens. Howe surpasses the record held by retired great Maurice "Rocket" Richard who scored his 544th goal in his 978th game. Howe required 1,132 games to attain the new record.

11

President Kennedy commemorates **Veterans Day** by placing a wreath on the Tomb of the Unknown Soldier at Arlington National Cemetery.

12

The U.S. Internal Revenue Service reports that $105.9 billion in **federal taxes** was collected in the fiscal year 1963.

According to A.C. Nielsen the **Top 5 Watched TV Shows** are:
1) The Beverly Hillbillies
2) Bonanza
3) The Dick Van Dyke Show
4) Petticoat Junction
5) The Andy Griffith Show

13

The Broadway play **"One Flew Over The Cuckoo's Nest"** opens in N.Y.C. The play is a study about life in a mental hospital, starring Kirk Douglas, Joan Tetzel, Ed Ames, and Gene Wilder in a supporting role. A very successful movie based on the story will be released during 1975, starring Jack Nicholson.

14

Robert O'Brien of MGM gives permission to go ahead and invest $12 million dollars for the film **"Dr. Zhivago"**. The movie, once released, will go on to make $47 million for the studio, helping to offset the company's losses of previous years.

15

The leading men's **PGA tour money-winner** for the second successive year, is Arnold Palmer with a record $128,230 in purse winnings. The women's winner, for the third consecutive year, is Mickey Wright with $31,269 in total winnings.

16

From The Hit Parade:
Gerry and The Pacemakers' hit **"You'll Never Walk Alone"** is the #1 pop single in the United Kingdom and will remain in top spot for the next 5 weeks until it is replaced by The Beatles' hit "She Loves You".

TV Programs Tonight On ABC:
7:30 Hootenanny
8:30 The Lawrence Welk Show
9:30 The Jerry Lewis Show

17

The Buick Motor Car Company's new **Riviera**, a hardtop coupe with up to 340 horsepower, sells at a base advertised price of $4,423.

The average cost of purchasing **precious metal** during this year is $35 for an ounce of gold and $1.28 for an ounce of silver.

18

United Artists release the star-studded film, **"It's A Mad, Mad, Mad, Mad World"**. A few of the many stars appearing in the movie are Spencer Tracy, Milton Berle, Sid Caesar, Buddy Hackett, Ethel Merman, Mickey Rooney, Phil Silvers, Terry Thomas, Jonathan Winters and Edie Adams.

19

The **National Cemetery** at Gettysburg, Pennsylvania, is re-dedicated on the 100th anniversary of its original dedication by Abraham Lincoln. President Kennedy, in a message, says *"The goals of liberty and freedom, the obligations of keeping ours a government of and for the people, are never ending"*.

20

Columbia Pictures releases the film **"Under The Yum Yum Tree"** with screenplay by Lawrence Roman, based on his play. The movie stars Jack Lemmon, Carol Lynley, Dean Jones, Edie Adams, Imogene Coca, Paul Lynde and Robert Lansing.

The #1 song in the United States is **"Deep Purple"** by Nino Tempo and April Steven.

21

President Kennedy arrives in San Antonio, to begin a two-day tour of Texas. The President dedicates the Aerospace Medical Health Centre near San Antonio. **Tomorrow morning, in the last speech** that the President will make in Ft. Worth he will say "This is a dangerous and uncertain world....We would like to live as we once lived but history will not permit it".

22

President John F. Kennedy, 46, is **assassinated** in Dallas, Texas. Struck in the head and neck by two bullets while riding in a motorcade, the President is pronounced dead at 1:00 pm at the Parkland Hospital. At 2:15 pm, police arrest Lee Harvey Oswald at the Texas Theater, six blocks from the scene. Vice-President Lyndon Baines Johnson, 55, is sworn in as the 36th President at 2:39 pm aboard the Presidential jet at Love Field in Dallas.

23

In the East Room of the White House, the **coffin of John F. Kennedy lays** on the catafalque where the body of Abraham Lincoln had reposed after his assassination. Members of his family, including his wife Jacqueline, daughter Caroline, 6, and John Jr. 3, then officials and dignitaries, pay their respects.

24

Despite apparent heavy security, arrested assassin-suspect of the President, **Lee Harvey Oswald**, 24, is shot and killed by Dallas night club owner Jack Ruby, 52, during a nationally-televised jail transfer.

Despite considerable criticism, the NFL **decides to play** its scheduled games. Many believe the league should have cancelled the games while the nation mourns the loss of its President.

25

Kings, Presidents and other high-ranking representatives of some 100 countries gather at **Arlington National Cemetery** for the funeral of the late President Kennedy. Mrs. Kennedy and the late President's two brothers Robert and Ted, light a symbolic eternal flame at the head of the grave.

26

From The Hit Parade:
The #1 song on the pop charts in the United States is **"I'm Leaving It Up To You"** by Dale and Grace.

Jack Ruby is indicted for murder in the shooting of Lee Harvey Oswald.

27

The **worst crash** in Canada's aviation history occurs when a Trans-Canada 4-engine DC-8F en route to Toronto crashes, minutes after takeoff from Montreal International Airport, killing all 118 people on board.

Musician **Jim Hendrix** celebrates his 21st birthday.

28

President Johnson, in a **Thanksgiving address** televised to the nation from the White House, pledges "to work for a new American greatness". The President announces that Cape Canaveral, Florida, will be renamed **Cape Kennedy** and the space installations will become the John F. Kennedy Space Center.

29

President Johnson appoints a **special commission** headed by **Chief Justice Earl Warren** to investigate President Kennedy's assassination. He instructs the commission *"to satisfy itself that the truth is known as far as it can be discovered and to report its findings and conclusions to him, to the American people, and to the world"*.

30

Soviet Ambassador to the U.S., Anatoly F. Dobrynin, turns over a sheaf of documents from the U.S.S.R.'s consular files on Lee H. Oswald to U.S. State Secretary Dean Rusk, who forwards them to the State Department. There is much speculation that Oswald may have shot the President on Soviet instructions.

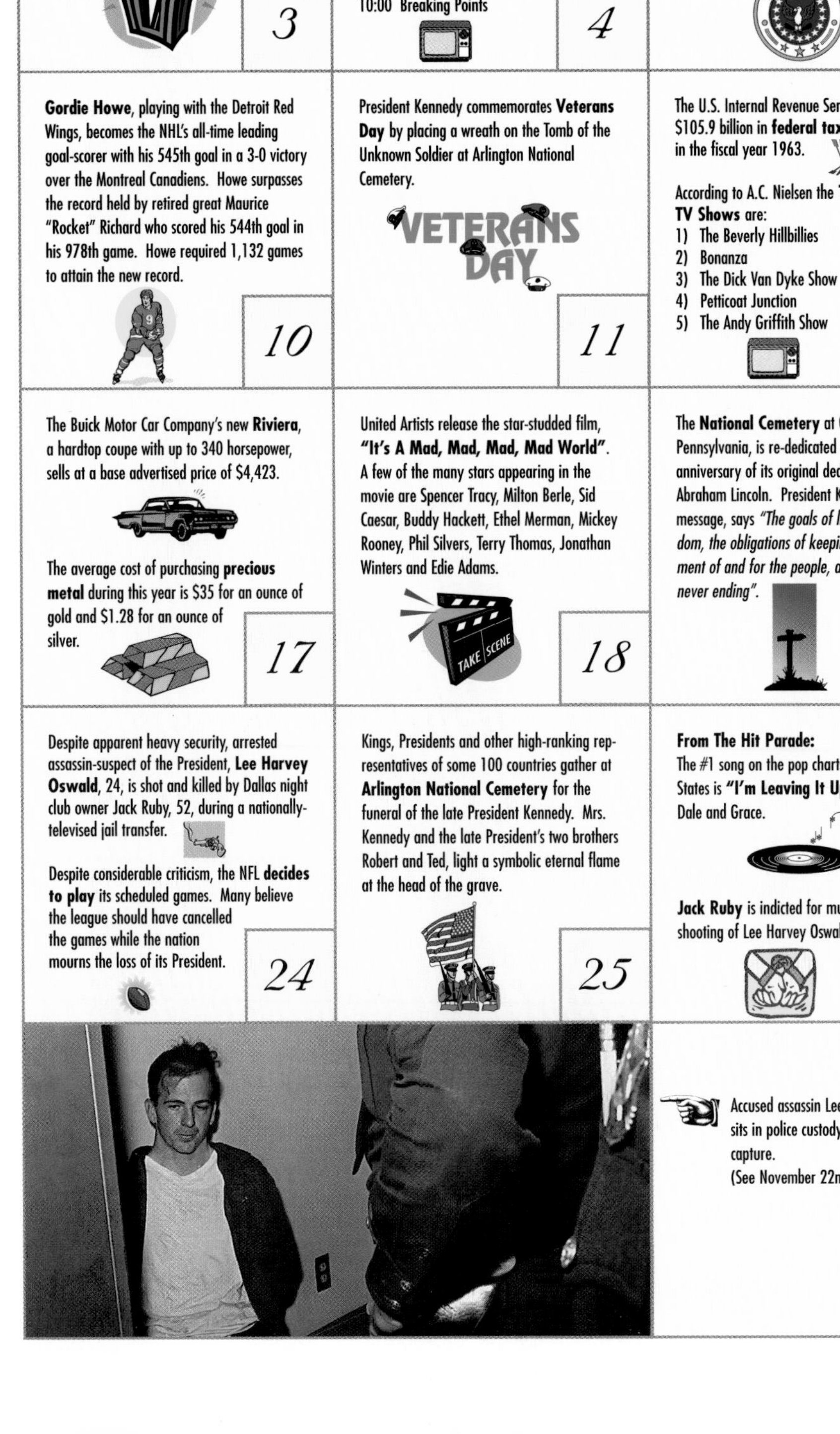

Accused assassin Lee Harvey Oswald sits in police custody following his capture.
(See November 22nd)

Peter, Paul and Mary top the Album Music Chart with their hit LP "In The Wind".
(See November 3rd)

1963 Buick Riviera 

DECEMBER 1963

Formula One driver Jim Clark wins the 1963 World Driving Championship.

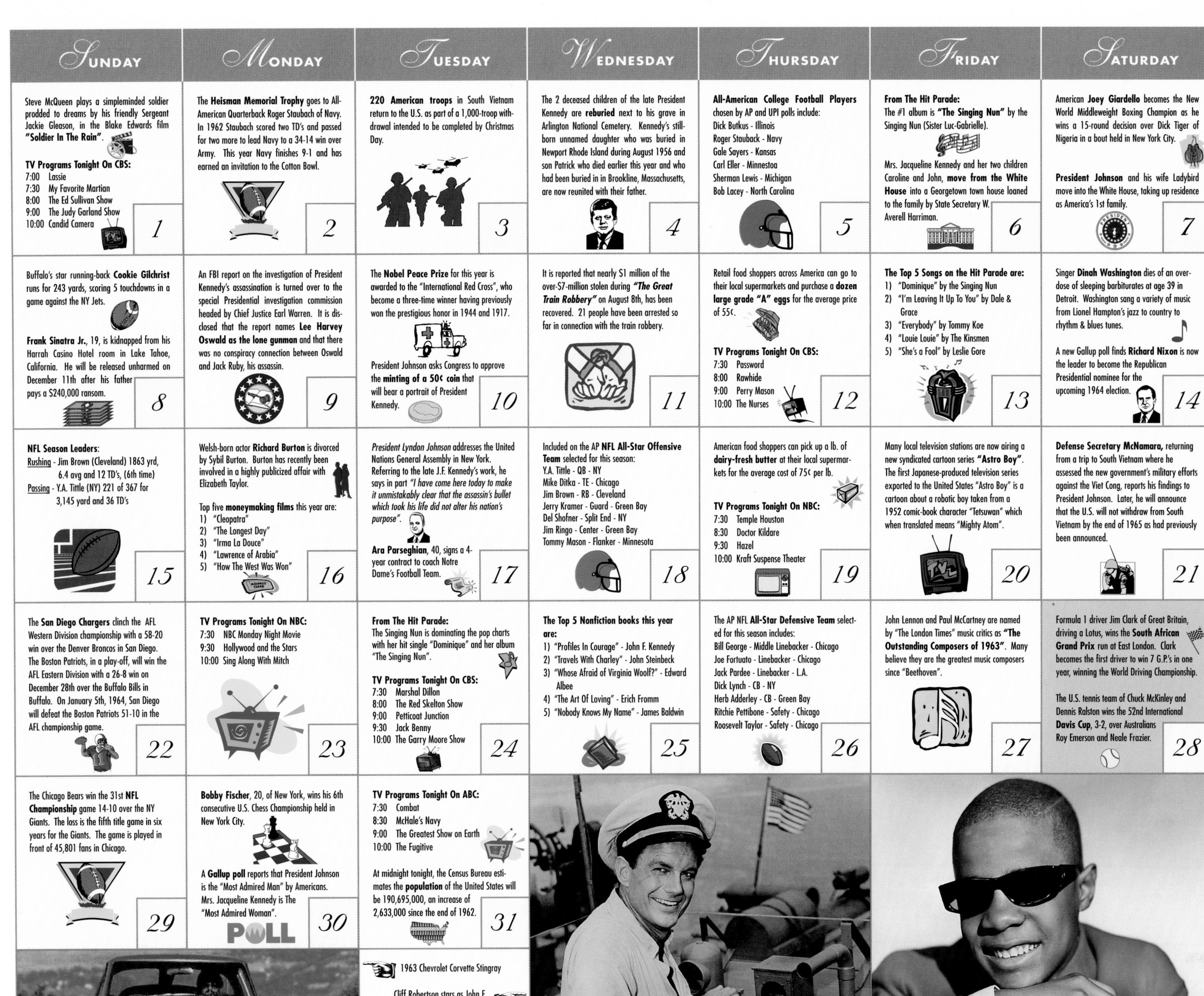

Sunday	Monday	Tuesday	Wednesday	Thursday	Friday	Saturday

1 — Steve McQueen plays a simpleminded soldier prodded to dreams by his friendly Sergeant Jackie Gleason, in the Blake Edwards film **"Soldier In The Rain"**.

TV Programs Tonight On CBS:
7:00 Lassie
7:30 My Favorite Martian
8:00 The Ed Sullivan Show
9:00 The Judy Garland Show
10:00 Candid Camera

2 — The **Heisman Memorial Trophy** goes to All-American Quarterback Roger Staubach of Navy. In 1962 Staubach scored two TD's and passed for two more to lead Navy to a 34-14 win over Army. This year Navy finishes 9-1 and has earned an invitation to the Cotton Bowl.

3 — **220 American troops** in South Vietnam return to the U.S. as part of a 1,000-troop withdrawal intended to be completed by Christmas Day.

4 — The 2 deceased children of the late President Kennedy are **reburied** next to his grave in Arlington National Cemetery. Kennedy's stillborn unnamed daughter who was buried in Newport Rhode Island during August 1956 and son Patrick who died earlier this year and who had been buried in in Brookline, Massachusetts, are now reunited with their father.

5 — **All-American College Football Players** chosen by AP and UPI polls include:
Dick Butkus - Illinois
Roger Stauback - Navy
Gale Sayers - Kansas
Carl Eller - Minnestoa
Sherman Lewis - Michigan
Bob Lacey - North Carolina

6 — **From The Hit Parade:**
The #1 album is **"The Singing Nun"** by the Singing Nun (Sister Luc-Gabrielle).

Mrs. Jacqueline Kennedy and her two children Caroline and John, **move from the White House** into a Georgetown town house loaned to the family by State Secretary W. Averell Harriman.

7 — American **Joey Giardello** becomes the New World Middleweight Boxing Champion as he wins a 15-round decision over Dick Tiger of Nigeria in a bout held in New York City.

President Johnson and his wife Ladybird move into the White House, taking up residence as America's 1st family.

8 — Buffalo's star running-back **Cookie Gilchrist** runs for 243 yards, scoring 5 touchdowns in a game against the NY Jets.

Frank Sinatra Jr., 19, is kidnapped from his Harrah Casino Hotel room in Lake Tahoe, California. He will be released unharmed on December 11th after his father pays a $240,000 ransom.

9 — An FBI report on the investigation of President Kennedy's assassination is turned over to the special Presidential investigation commission headed by Chief Justice Earl Warren. It is disclosed that the report names **Lee Harvey Oswald as the lone gunman** and that there was no conspiracy connection between Oswald and Jack Ruby, his assassin.

10 — The **Nobel Peace Prize** for this year is awarded to the "International Red Cross", who become a three-time winner having previously won the prestigious honor in 1944 and 1917.

President Johnson asks Congress to approve the **minting of a 50¢ coin** that will bear a portrait of President Kennedy.

11 — It is reported that nearly $1 million of the over-$7-million stolen during ***"The Great Train Robbery"*** on August 8th, has been recovered. 21 people have been arrested so far in connection with the train robbery.

12 — Retail food shoppers across America can go to their local supermarkets and purchase a **dozen large grade "A" eggs** for the average price of 55¢.

TV Programs Tonight On CBS:
7:30 Password
8:00 Rawhide
9:00 Perry Mason
10:00 The Nurses

13 — **The Top 5 Songs on the Hit Parade are:**
1) "Dominique" by the Singing Nun
2) "I'm Leaving It Up To You" by Dale & Grace
3) "Everybody" by Tommy Koe
4) "Louie Louie" by The Kinsmen
5) "She's a Fool" by Leslie Gore

14 — Singer **Dinah Washington** dies of an overdose of sleeping barbiturates at age 39 in Detroit. Washington sang a variety of music from Lionel Hampton's jazz to country to rhythm & blues tunes.

A new Gallup poll finds **Richard Nixon** is now the leader to become the Republican Presidential nominee for the upcoming 1964 election.

15 — **NFL Season Leaders**:
Rushing - Jim Brown (Cleveland) 1863 yrd, 6.4 avg and 12 TD's, (6th time)
Passing - Y.A. Tittle (NY) 221 of 367 for 3,145 yard and 36 TD's

16 — Welsh-born actor **Richard Burton** is divorced by Sybil Burton. Burton has recently been involved in a highly publicized affair with Elizabeth Taylor.

Top five **moneymaking films** this year are:
1) "Cleopatra"
2) "The Longest Day"
3) "Irma La Douce"
4) "Lawrence of Arabia"
5) "How The West Was Won"

17 — *President Lyndon Johnson* addresses the United Nations General Assembly in New York. Referring to the late J.F. Kennedy's work, he says in part *"I have come here today to make it unmistakably clear that the assassin's bullet which took his life did not alter his nation's purpose"*.

Ara Parseghian, 40, signs a 4-year contract to coach Notre Dame's Football Team.

18 — Included on the AP **NFL All-Star Offensive Team** selected for this season:
Y.A. Tittle - QB - NY
Mike Ditka - TE - Chicago
Jim Brown - RB - Cleveland
Jerry Kramer - Guard - Green Bay
Del Shofner - Split End - NY
Jim Ringo - Center - Green Bay
Tommy Mason - Flanker - Minnesota

19 — American food shoppers can pick up a lb. of **dairy-fresh butter** at their local supermarkets for the average cost of 75¢ per lb.

TV Programs Tonight On NBC:
7:30 Temple Houston
8:30 Doctor Kildare
9:30 Hazel
10:00 Kraft Suspense Theater

20 — Many local television stations are now airing a new syndicated cartoon series **"Astro Boy"**. The first Japanese-produced television series exported to the United States "Astro Boy" is a cartoon about a robotic boy taken from a 1952 comic-book character "Tetsuwan" which when translated means "Mighty Atom".

21 — **Defense Secretary McNamara,** returning from a trip to South Vietnam where he assessed the new government's military efforts against the Viet Cong, reports his findings to President Johnson. Later, he will announce that the U.S. will not withdraw from South Vietnam by the end of 1965 as had previously been announced.

22 — The **San Diego Chargers** clinch the AFL Western Division championship with a 58-20 win over the Denver Broncos in San Diego. The Boston Patriots, in a play-off, will win the AFL Eastern Division with a 26-8 win on December 28th over the Buffalo Bills in Buffalo. On January 5th, 1964, San Diego will defeat the Boston Patriots 51-10 in the AFL championship game.

23 — **TV Programs Tonight On NBC:**
7:30 NBC Monday Night Movie
9:30 Hollywood and the Stars
10:00 Sing Along With Mitch

24 — **From The Hit Parade:**
The Singing Nun is dominating the pop charts with her hit single "Dominique" and her album "The Singing Nun".

TV Programs Tonight On CBS:
7:30 Marshal Dillon
8:00 The Red Skelton Show
9:00 Petticoat Junction
9:30 Jack Benny
10:00 The Garry Moore Show

25 — **The Top 5 Nonfiction books this year are:**
1) "Profiles In Courage" - John F. Kennedy
2) "Travels With Charley" - John Steinbeck
3) "Whose Afraid of Virginia Woolf?" - Edward Albee
4) "The Art Of Loving" - Erich Fromm
5) "Nobody Knows My Name" - James Baldwin

26 — The AP NFL **All-Star Defensive Team** selected for this season includes:
Bill George - Middle Linebacker - Chicago
Joe Fortuato - Linebacker - Chicago
Jack Pardee - Linebacker - L.A.
Dick Lynch - CB - NY
Herb Adderley - CB - Green Bay
Ritchie Pettibone - Safety - Chicago
Roosevelt Taylor - Safety - Chicago

27 — John Lennon and Paul McCartney are named by "The London Times" music critics as **"The Outstanding Composers of 1963"**. Many believe they are the greatest music composers since "Beethoven".

28 — Formula 1 driver Jim Clark of Great Britain, driving a Lotus, wins the **South African Grand Prix** run at East London. Clark becomes the first driver to win 7 G.P.'s in one year, winning the World Driving Championship.

The U.S. tennis team of Chuck McKinley and Dennis Ralston wins the 52nd International **Davis Cup**, 3-2, over Australians Roy Emerson and Neale Frazier.

29 — The Chicago Bears win the 31st **NFL Championship** game 14-10 over the NY Giants. The loss is the fifth title game in six years for the Giants. The game is played in front of 45,801 fans in Chicago.

30 — **Bobby Fischer**, 20, of New York, wins his 6th consecutive U.S. Chess Championship held in New York City.

A **Gallup poll** reports that President Johnson is the "Most Admired Man" by Americans. Mrs. Jacqueline Kennedy is The "Most Admired Woman".

31 — **TV Programs Tonight On ABC:**
7:30 Combat
8:30 McHale's Navy
9:00 The Greatest Show on Earth
10:00 The Fugitive

At midnight tonight, the Census Bureau estimates the **population** of the United States will be 190,695,000, an increase of 2,633,000 since the end of 1962.

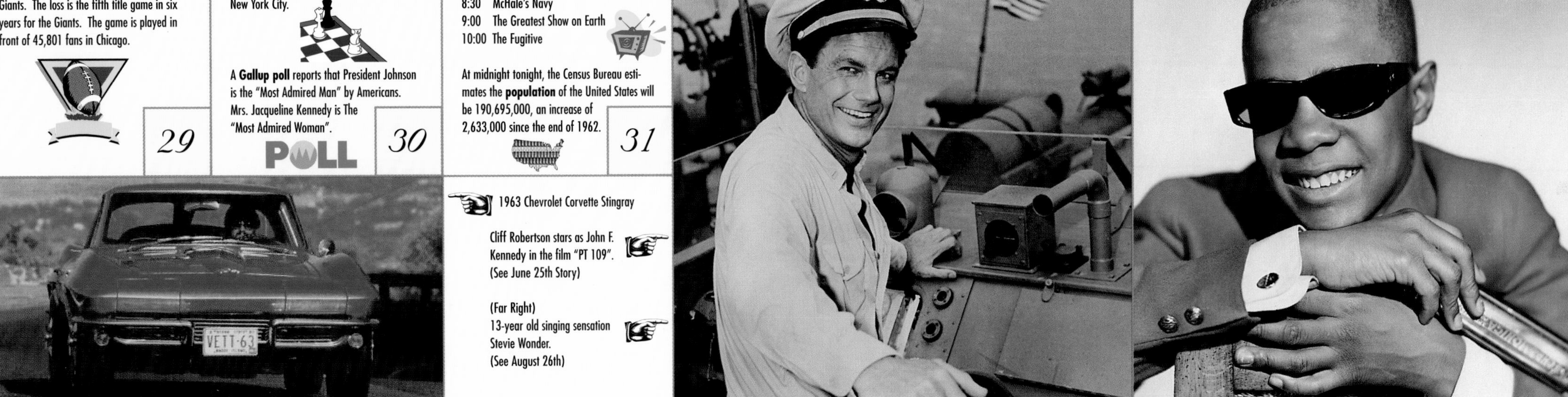

1963 Chevrolet Corvette Stingray

Cliff Robertson stars as John F. Kennedy in the film "PT 109". (See June 25th Story)

(Far Right)
13-year old singing sensation Stevie Wonder.
(See August 26th)

USA
NASA
Atlantis